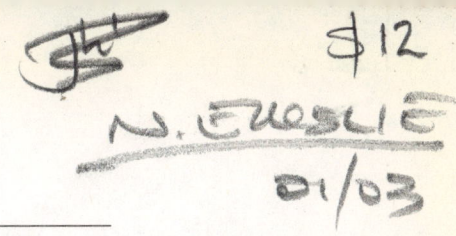

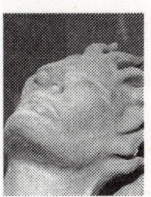

Faces of the Goddess

New Zealand women talk
about their spirituality

Céline Kearney

TANDEM PRESS

The photographic images used throughout this book are details from sculptures by Helen Pollock. In order of appearance they are: 'Altar' (1992, artist's collection), 'Observance II' (1995, private collection), 'Medial' (1994, private collection), 'Observance IV' (1995, private collection)

First published in New Zealand in 1997 by
TANDEM PRESS
2 Rugby Road, Birkenhead, North Shore City
New Zealand

ISBN 1 877178 04 7

DESIGN AND PRODUCTION BY MOSCOW DESIGN

PRINTED AND BOUND BY AUSTRALIAN PRINT GROUP

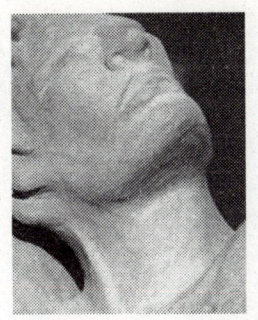

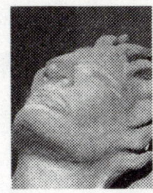

CONTENTS

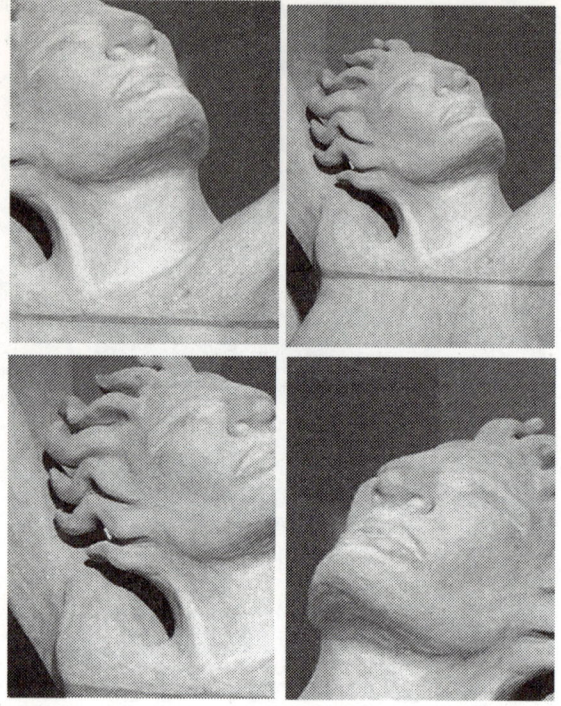

INTRODUCTION

ABOUT 10 YEARS AGO I HAD A CONVERSATION IN WHICH I WAS TOLD
THAT WOMEN INVOLVED IN DEVELOPING THEIR SPIRITUALITY WERE
NOT DEALING WITH 'REAL ISSUES' IN THE 'REAL WORLD'.
TAKEN ABACK BY WHAT SEEMED A STUNNINGLY INSULAR MENTALITY
I DIDN'T BOTHER ASKING WHAT THE 'REAL ISSUES'
WERE CONSIDERED TO BE.

Granted, awareness of and debate about spirituality in the women's movement were reasonably new to New Zealand then, but women in Europe,
in Germany for instance, had been writing about their experiences for
over 20 years, some preceding women in England and the United States

who had been writing about this for two decades, perhaps more.

In these contexts I'm thinking of Western women's experience and ideas about spirituality. As a New Zealander I can look from these Western cultures to indigenous Maori and Pacific Island cultures where women have lived their spiritual traditions for centuries as an integral part of their societies and communities, though dislocated at times by the effects of colonisation.

I therefore decided to talk to women who are developing their spirituality to see how it related to their lives. I decided to interview women only as a way of balancing the time and energy I'd already used focusing on theology written by men and on patriarchal institutions. I chose for the most part not to interview women who take an active part in mainstream religious institutions. However, there are articulate women within these institutions who have their own stories to tell, women whose strength and creativity are a real challenge for change.

I felt strongly at the time of that conversation, as I still do, that spirituality is about 'real issues' for women and men. I also feel that being involved in women's spirituality is a challenge to a fundamental belief that underpins the whole of Western society and which has been responsible for enormous oppression, primarily of women: that God the source of all life is exclusively male.

Thankfully, the attitude to spirituality within the women's movement and wider New Zealand society has changed a great deal over the past 10 years or so. There is an enormous amount happening both inside mainstream religious institutions and in different networks around the country for both women and men.

I was brought up Roman Catholic – Irish Catholic – as was all my family for at least four generations on both sides of the family, two of these generations being in New Zealand.

We lived on a farm on the east coast of the South Island, just outside Oamaru. The land, the sea and the mountains were an important part of my childhood and I can clearly remember as a child sitting on top of a hill, the sea behind me and the mountains in the distance in front with the sky streaked red at sunset, feeling a part of all this, connected at an unconscious level.

Until I was 16 my life was defined by the cycle of lambing, shearing, harvesting, summer holidays of picking potatoes and the changes of the weather from drought to bitter snow wind. I went to a Catholic school, belonged to a Catholic parish and had a circle of family and friends who were almost all Catholic. I used to enjoy the peace and quiet of the church as a place to think and be still.

I enjoyed my schooling by the Dominican Sisters, educated women who encouraged us as young women to extend ourselves and develop our abilities. My mother's sister is a Dominican sister so there are strong links between the Dominican community and the family, and for me a great deal of kindness and affection.

My mother, although a devout Catholic, also had Germaine Greer's *The Female Eunuch* and Mary Daly's *The Church and the Second Sex* on the bookshelf at home while I was at secondary school. I grew up in what I felt was an intellectually open environment, though my father has never quite recovered from the first onslaught of feminism in a household of four daughters and a youngest son. On the strength of her convictions my mother had started a branch of SPUC (Society for the Protection of the Unborn Child) in Oamaru, so I also grew up being quite familiar with the material they produced.

In my first year at university in Dunedin I used to come home and lie on the grass and feel centred again after living in the city. Being part of the Catholic Society on campus was socially and intellectually stimulating as we organised speakers and attended discussions.

After graduating and working on my home-town newspaper for a year I found I wasn't interested in the rounds of daily journalism. I went to Auckland to work as a journalist for the national Catholic newspaper, which then had a liberal editorial policy with quite an emphasis on social justice. Not finding a niche there, I later worked as a peace educator for the Catholic Diocese of Auckland, as well as continuing to freelance for other publications, three years with a magazine for and about disabled people. I did some writing for the national 'pro-life' newspaper and some work with Pregnancy Help, believing that if women wanted to have a baby and needed support there should be support available to them.

In the very early eighties I was active in the peace movement, working to have New Zealand declared nuclear-free and writing about issues concerning the nuclearisation of the Pacific and the related struggles of indigenous peoples in the Nuclear Free and Independent Pacific movement. With four Irish Catholic grandparents I understood how Ireland had been colonised over a period of about 700 years, but working in the NFIP movement I came to understand for the first time how I was a part of a process that colonised Maori in this land. The irony still strikes me that people escaping poverty in one country can help create much the same situation for another group of people in another country.

In those years I found the synthesis of the church's writings on social justice and individual theologians' writings on liberation theology very stimulating and particularly enjoyed the humour and breadth of creation spirituality.

I worked with and hosted people whose Catholicism was closely connected to their work for social change and for 'justice' – they were people of courage and integrity from various church communities in Auckland, other parts of New Zealand and around the world. But these men and women and their strong lives didn't change the institutional treatment of women, particularly its denial of an equal public role for them in ministry. I read a lot of women's theology and was active in groups trying to change the institutional attitude towards women, but I felt that the struggle for change was going to be too long and too hard.

...WORKING IN THE NFIP MOVEMENT I CAME TO UNDERSTAND FOR THE FIRST TIME HOW I WAS PART OF A PROCESS THAT COLONISED MAORI IN THIS LAND.

There seemed to me to be no 'justice' for women within the institution. The church which had been a place of sanctuary for me became a place of tension and unhappiness.

It cost me a lot to walk away from a community – an international community, a whole culture – that had shaped me and of which I felt so deeply a part, but I could not mentally or physically bear the struggle any longer. I gave most of my theology books to one of my sisters. But my spirituality was important to me, and my involvement in the peace movement had provided me with a situation in which I could continue to explore and express it.

During two years in Ireland, England and parts of Europe I had continually returned to Greenham Common women's peace camp in England and spent three months at a women's peace camp in Geneva observing the United Nations Disarmament Conference. In these situations I had had powerful experiences of the use of ritual and symbols.

Greenham Common Airforce Base was in those years – 1984-85 –home to American Cruise missiles and land-based nuclear warheads. Women had set up camps, each named for a colour of the rainbow, around the 14-

kilometre fence and women from around England and the world came to spend time there as a protest against the global nuclear arms build-up. New Zealanders and Australians tended to congregate at Green Gate, off the road in the forest.

Women who lived at the camp and those who came to visit put up pictures, posters, banners and symbols of their children and the people they loved who would die in a nuclear war. The fence was routinely stripped, but while the images lasted they were powerful symbols of the human spirit claiming life in the face of death. Sunflowers bloomed for a while in one of the camps on the grass verge between the wire fence and the highway, symbols of life and hope in the face of huge, death-dealing forces.

I found the visual images, symbols and rituals at Greenham Common very powerful. One particularly powerful ritual was when we stood in a long line in the late afternoon facing the high wire fence keening – wailing in grief – for those who would die in a nuclear explosion. The sound of our wailing echoed back into the forest and across the open spaces inside the fence.

Another ritual took place on Waitangi Day 1985. We were three or four New Zealand women who had agreed to meet at Greenham to mark that day with none of the ritual planned beforehand. We met at Green Gate and in a clearing made a map of New Zealand with small rocks and stones. Then we walked around the whole 'country' several times in single file in silence, thinking of what Waitangi Day meant for us and placing small candles on any area of the country that related to this. I remember putting candles on Taranaki to mark Parihaka Marae and on Auckland for Bastion Point, as they were places of struggle that I was familiar with. As the late afternoon drew on we sat and talked about where and why we had placed our candles. Then we put other candles wherever we felt we wanted to. I put mine on the Mackenzie Country and Central Otago, places where the land and the lakes are very powerful for me, and on Auckland where I lived. We explained again where and why we placed our candles and sat in silence watching the candles until dark.

After my experience of ritual, which had been mostly in the context of direct action for political and social change, when I returned to Auckland I attended two courses on ritual-making run by Juliet Batten. Out of those courses grew Aurora women's ritual group which has been meeting – with changes of members – ever since. From those courses and the rituals we've done marking the eight sabbats and other personal occasions I have developed an understanding of the rhythm of the seasons, of a time for growth and activity and also of the need to withdraw inward physically and be less active. So I now have a model in my own life for a way out of a tendency to burn out because of prolonged action. This view of life also helps me to enjoy life and have fun, which was something I had forgotten about.

Several years later I did a course with Lea Holford on mythology which looked at the core symbols and myths of the major world religions. I've found now I have a real interest in mythology and stories from different cultures.

I FOUND THE VISUAL IMAGES, SYMBOLS AND RITUALS AT GREENHAM COMMON VERY POWERFUL... THE SOUND OF OUR WAILING ECHOED BACK INTO THE FOREST AND ACROSS THE OPEN SPACES INSIDE THE FENCE.

✧

I've never wanted to substitute the 'Goddess' for 'God' but I feel much happier celebrating the cycle of the seasons and with a cyclical view of life which is integrally a part of the ancient pre-Christian European Wiccan traditions on which the rituals are based. Though I live in a large city, following the yearly cycle of the rituals keeps me aware of the seasons and the moon. I find winter difficult, but the autumn equinox, Samhain and winter solstice rituals make the dark and cold more tolerable because I'm reminded the season will turn.

After such an intense intellectual effort to make all the pieces fit into a theoretical synthesis in Roman Catholicism I've had little mental energy for an in-depth analysis of the Wiccan tradition or the history/herstory of individual goddesses and their archetypes. My overwhelming physical, emotional and psychological need has been to get out of my head, back into my body and feel some kind of balance with the different aspects of myself as a whole and to enjoy the connection that I have always felt with this land.

As I get some emotional distance from the institution I can see it can be destructive for men too, that we are all daughters and sons of patriarchy. No doubt my liking for a tradition where the female is honoured as an individual entity, and a very powerful one at that, is a reaction to God the Father and the male hierarchy of the Church of Rome. But I still feel very comfortable with the Holy Spirit as a creative spirit which enlivens everything from the tiniest atom to the entire cosmos.

My experience of women's spirituality is that it offers access not only to images of women and the feminine as divine but also images of what it is to be male and masculine.

I know that much of the Roman Catholic tradition is still very deeply a part of my psyche and that there were a lot of positive things in it for me as I grew up. Several of the books I didn't give away and still feel comfortable with are about the experience of prayer and meditation: some of the writings of the thirteenth-century mystic, Mechtild of Magdeburg; the story of Catherine de Hueck Doherty about the Russian spiritual tradition of the Poustinia; and an Irish Trappist monk writing about prayer. To me these are essentially about what the process of ritual allows for me – a physical and psychological space for meditation.

I support my nephews and nieces in their Christian and Catholic education because I feel it's good for them to know their own tradition as a place to stand. But I also share my experiences from my ritual group to show them a wider view of spirituality than the one they are learning and living. I've given some of them a book of creation stories from many cultures, to help widen their perspective and show them that God has many names and many faces.

After spending almost a year in Ireland I feel I can draw on my own Celtic traditions. I particularly enjoy celebrating Brigid, on August 1, at Candlemas, the fire festival of increasing light. Brigid was the ancient Irish goddess of fire and a triple goddess of smithcraft, poetry and healing. I can use the St Brigid's Cross, made of reeds, which I got in Londonderry and which I saw my own cousins – twice removed – make in Tipperary. The cross, a symbol of protection from harm, is a link with the ancient Celtic tradition that survives today. Recently in Auckland I did a weekend with Nicola Campbell and Peta Joyce which provided insight into the Celtic world view and Celtic spirituality. This is an area I shall continue to explore. I also enjoy the Dances of Universal Peace which Laurie Ross teaches in Auckland. For me they are like a meditation in movement.

My understanding and experience of spirituality keeps developing and I feel free.

✧

THE WOMEN INCLUDED IN THIS COLLECTION ARE:

◈

BARBARA STANLEY, a community-based mental health worker who has been involved for a number of years with organising an older women's festival on Auckland's North Shore.

LEA HOLFORD is a psychologist who tutored a women's spirituality course at Auckland University Continuing Education for seven years and has also tutored a variety of other classes connected to spirituality and psychology.

HINEWIRANGI KOHU of Ngati Kahungunu and Ngati Rongomai Wahine is a poet, writer and artist who draws deeply on her spiritual traditions. She shares one of her poems and a story.

NOREEN PENNY has been involved in making rituals in groups since 1981. She has published a book, *Women's Rites: An Alternative to Patriarchal Religion*, recording her experience of this and of some of the other women involved.

MARY HANCOCK is a ceremony and ritual-maker who sees her role as a facilitator empowering people to do what human beings can do innately – celebrate life's key transitions. In 1996 she established a training programme for celebrants and ritual-makers at the Auckland Institute of Technology.

RUTH TAI'S whanau are extended families from Tuhoe, Whakatohea, Ngai ti Rangi, Ngati Awa and Tuwharetoa (ki Kawerau) tribes. Through her writing, tapes and experiential workshops she is sharing the spiritual teachings she acquired as a child.

JANET MELBOURNE is a natural therapist and a teacher of yoga. She finds the absence of energy flow or blocks to the energy flow in the lives of her clients are often in an area of spirit, the area of passionate love of life, and in the sense of being part of a greater whole.

CATHIE DUNSFORD teaches writing and publishing at Auckland University and runs a publishing consultancy. Spirituality and creativity are deeply connected in her own life, and her novels and poetry are expressions of the spirituality she has put out into the world.

AUDREY SHARP lives in a rural community where she is developing an organic farm which she plans to set up as a place of retreat in the future. Audrey's politics and spirituality are integrally linked with her sense of social responsibility.

JULIET BATTEN is an artist, psychotherapist and writer who has found an interweaving between ritual, art and politics. She has spent several years teaching people to create ritual.

RUTH GARDNER has through her own initial experience of being involved in ritual groups been able to offer others an experience of ritual and women's spirituality through a variety of situations. She currently manages a volunteer centre in Christchurch.

RAEWYNNE, who has chosen not to be identified by her surname, teaches ancient Egyptian and Greek mythologies and the ritual techniques of both of these, as well as basic ritual technique crystal healing. She has been aided in this and in other aspects of her life by archetypal beings, spirit teachers.

HELEN POLLOCK is a potter and sculptor whose work includes images of the feminine. She believes it is empowering for women to see images of themselves as strong divine beings.

Many of these women are drawing upon knowledge that has been available for millennia, some of which has been suppressed, replaced or forgotten in different times, places and cultures. They are reshaping it and using it in their lives in New Zealand now.

All these traditions and many more are available to us: the practices and beliefs of the Wiccan tradition of Pre-Christian Europe; the Celtic traditions which are the heritage of many New Zealanders; the Mystics of the Christian tradition; the deities and practices of the Buddhist tradition; the traditions of indigenous peoples of this land and from other Pacific cultures, and others not touched on in these interviews.

We have an opportunity to learn from these traditions and with respect use what we need or what we can to live compassionately and creatively.

BARBARA STANLEY

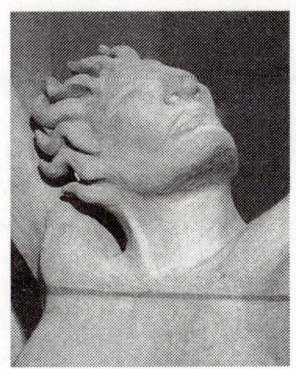

THE WEST COAST SURF ROLLS ONTO THE BEACH, BREAKERS WHIPPED
BY THE WIND. A GROUP OF WOMEN STAND ON THE ROCKS
BELOW THE HEADLAND AND THROW ASHES FROM THE
PREVIOUS NIGHT'S RITUAL INTO THE SEA.
THEIR FEARS FOR THE DARKNESS OF THE WINTER AND THEIR OWN
PERSONAL DARKNESS ARE SYMBOLICALLY CARRIED AWAY WITH THE WIND
AND THE TIDE.

Barbara and the women in her ritual group have gathered to mark the winter solstice, June 21, the longest night of the year: a time to face the darkness without and within. By facing their fears and expressing them they hope to move through them to face the future with new energy and strength.

During the ritual the women have sat in silence for a time, then written or drawn or made a symbol of the darkness they faced and thrown this into the fire, leaving it to burn to ashes. As a symbol of their new freedom they each throw a handful of the ashes into the sea the next morning.

Samhain, April 30, known as Halloween, also All Souls Eve, is a time to remember the dead. Barbara has prepared the ritual centrepiece. In the centre of the room she has set a large bowl filled with earth and dotted with roses. It is surrounded by pictures of a Latin American Day of the

Dead celebration, where people dress up as skeletons and ghosts and have a riotously good time.

She has marked the four geographical points of north, south, east and west with symbols: a red candle for north, symbolising fire; stones and petrified wood for south, symbolising earth; a bowl of water and shells for west, symbolising water; and feathers and burning incense for east, symbolising air.

The women bring a picture or a symbol of someone or something that has died, and a candle to light and put in the centre bowl among the roses after they have talked about their symbol or picture. They gather around the centrepiece and sit comfortably. Barbara, who is leading the ritual, invites them to join hands for a moment to 'cast the circle', marking the physical space in which the ritual takes place and establishing that the time for the ritual has begun. 'The circle is cast. We are between the worlds, where night and day meet as one,' she says in a clear voice.

Barbara, mother of eight children and several grandchildren, is a strong, vital woman in her late sixties. She lives on Auckland's North Shore with her husband and is a field worker at a local community mental health centre.

Born in Auckland and brought up a Catholic, her mother's death when she was 13 shook her confidence in what the nuns were teaching her. Although he was not Catholic her father continued to take the children to Mass and to send them to Catholic boarding schools.

After leaving school she went nursing, became friends with a strongly agnostic family and stopped going to Mass at the age of 19.

Barbara was married in a registry office, which was unusual for a woman of her generation as most of her contemporaries were married in a church even if they did not have religious beliefs.

For a number of years she has helped organise an older women's festival on the North Shore. *The Circle Is Cast*, a collection of poetry and images by Barbara and Lenore Webster, was published in 1996. The collection is about the empowerment women have felt in discovering goddesses, whether of the ancient world or of Aotearoa, and reflects archetypes and metaphors of the feminine.

I did Lea Holford's course on women's spirituality at Auckland University's Continuing Education in 1984. Through the course I realised very clearly that nature was part of us and we were part of it. We used symbols that stood for wholeness – earth, air, fire and water – which are part of our environment and our bodies; they are what made our children and will make our children's children.

I have found parallels between the experience of therapy and women's spirituality.

Lea's course was enormously influential for me. I think I was going through a traumatic time because of depression. One ritual I remember is where we all brought along something we wanted to heal in our lives. We didn't necessarily have to talk about it but if we wanted to we could move into the circle and sit there and be with it. It was very powerful and a lot of the power was to do with the silence and the fact that you allowed yourself to be there and experience whatever it was. I felt very much that we were healed by our ability to sit and be with it and by the touching and the connection we felt.

This and other rituals shifted me into a feminist stance in a way nothing else had. What women could do for each other was enormously moving. We didn't need priests – we had our own sense of power and our own sense of each other.

When I talked to other women in the group and we shared our stories, I realised how important it was to tell your story, to be heard and acknowledged and to be listened to with reverence and silence and to be honoured in the process. In a lot of our rituals we share a part of ourselves because we have to speak from the heart. Speaking from the heart is not something we are encouraged to do as Pakeha. You're supposed to polish things up and prepare it and speak from your head.

'THE CIRCLE IS CAST. WE ARE BETWEEN THE WORLDS, WHERE NIGHT AND DAY MEET AS ONE,' SHE SAYS IN A CLEAR VOICE.

I think what I learned as a child was that as a Catholic you had to wear a mask and that you were either good or bad – you couldn't just be yourself. In ritual I've been able to remove that mask, saying 'this is what it's been like for me', and other women have heard and acknowledged it. The fact of weeping with a group of women was such a powerful thing to do. And to use symbols – to pick up a stone and say 'my heart feels like this stone' – was also very powerful.

After Lea's course we formed our own group with initial help from women who were interested enough to help us experiment with six rituals. The 10 of us met for about two years, doing rituals about our mothers, our anger, our lives, learning how we could improve them, and how to cope better if we were in a relationship.

For me it was a very exciting thing to do. It was like a new dimension and it was a wonderful opportunity to be 'the priest'. For girls and young women being the priest was an enormous step to take.

After the rituals I have had a sense of being centred in an ancient religion from which I have just stepped out. I have been in pulpits and looked down and felt like a priest since then. After being a priestess in a ritual you could be one anywhere.

Many younger women from the group moved away and there wasn't enough to keep it going. I didn't know what to do at that stage; it had been such an exciting thing to come together as women and we had shared very deeply about our lives, that it seemed sad for us to go our separate ways again.

Women's spirituality – learning to work with women in a supportive environment – was a great shift for me. After talking about rituals and symbolism I realised there was an enormous number of symbols in my life, without the sense of the religiousness that the objects actually held. (The term 'religiousness' for me is not connected to 'God' but to beauty, the unknown, a sense of time, of speculation about life and the enormity of it.) I had collected beautiful stones and shells and driftwood as part of my sense of nature and of continuity. Lea's course seemed to highlight all these things.

I had a nightgown I'd never considered as being part of a ritual until I joined the women's spirituality group. My first child was born while I was wearing it and thereafter I wore this gown when giving birth to all of them. By the time my last child was born it was very ancient and threadbare. Having so many children has been quite a religious experience for me.

It was from developing an awareness of ritual in everyday life that I saw how many rituals there were. For me it is linked with a sense of beauty and awe. When I watch the gannets as they move, fly and dive at Muriwai Beach on Auckland's West Coast I am awed that they could be so beautiful. And with words as well: there is a feeling of power in a poem that moves me, in the words that convey or explain similar experiences.

I still find beauty in the rituals of the church, like the Mass in Latin and burning candles. There is still an essence there though it is quite immaterial that it is connected to a patriarchal God.

When I go into cathedrals in England and Europe I am aware of how ancient they are. I admire the people who built them rather than the God who inspired them. When I go into a church and there's music and people gathered together sharing, that's the ritual, rather than any sense of what's traditionally regarded as 'the spirit of God moving in me'.

I attended Juliet Batten's course in 1987. She enlarged on the use of ritual and was good at using symbols of this country, like native plants and trees, and she created rituals around issues that were important for us in Aotearoa/New Zealand.

Being involved in women's spirituality gives an opportunity for self-exploration that's not necessarily a therapy situation. It allows for consciousness-raising, which is what so many women have found helpful in feminism. Issues of spirituality, feminism and politics all merged when I discovered the way women's history has been buried and is being rediscovered in women's groups.

I don't mind being called a 'witch', but I think there are a lot of mistaken ideas about what being a witch really means. People's vision of a witch on a broomstick doing bad deeds results from the patriarchal viewpoint. I think witches are instruments of change, especially for women. The fear people have about witches touches the really primitive parts of their mind and I'm very distrustful of this. I think this fear has to be tempered by self-knowledge and the dark side of one's own personality needs to be owned and accepted; then the need to act out fears destructively as regards witches should disappear.

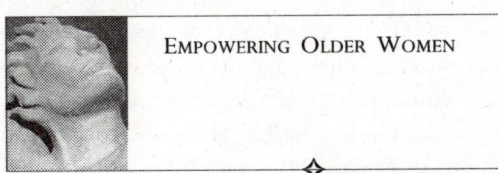

EMPOWERING OLDER WOMEN

My awareness of old age started when I spent a few years nursing in the Little Sisters of the Poor rest home in Herne Bay. I became aware of the awful dependency issues that were created in women who came into the rest home. They lost something of themselves, they were returned to being 'good girls', behaving as others told them to, so they lost their power – needlessly, I thought. I used to look at them and think if they'd had enough support they wouldn't have had to go into a rest home.

So that became my passion. I wondered what had happened in their lives; putting their name on a waiting list seemed quite crucial. If their name came up they were told if they didn't go into the rest home they might lose their position, which created fear. What would they do if they went to the bottom of the list?

I remember a remarkable woman of 90 who had been the centre of activity in her street in Central Auckland. A lot of the women in the street used to visit her, she knew them all and their children knew her. Then her name came up, so she thought about it and in the end her fear was too great and she went to live in the rest home. People from the street used to visit her for a while, then they slowly stopped coming. She had been removed from their lives and much as they loved her, once she was gone that was probably the end of their relationship with her.

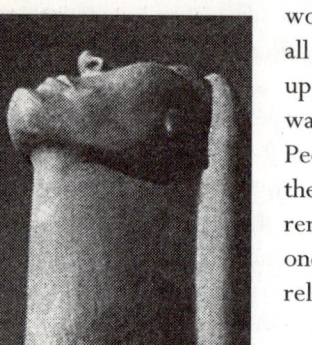

THE TANGATA WHENUA RECOGNISE THEIR OLD KUIA ARE THE WISE WOMEN; THIS WAS AN ATTEMPT TO HAVE SOMETHING FOR PAKEHA WOMEN, SINCE TO BE OLD AND PAKEHA IN NEW ZEALAND IS TO BE DISCREDITED.

I saw this person change from being a lively woman with a keen interest in everything to become like the other women in the home who sat and watched television. Nothing much happened in her life; it was such a contrast.

After I joined the community mental health network in Raeburn House on Auckland's North Shore, eventually an opportunity came up for me to work with older women. About eight years ago we advertised an older women's support group in the local paper and sent notices to doctors. Women came originally because they were depressed and they have kept coming. I think there are a lot of women who go through counselling or who go to their doctors; they could talk endlessly to these people, but then what? A support group seems the obvious answer.

As facilitators we listened to these women's stories and thought how amazing they were. All their lives seemed so interesting yet they had no sense of this themselves — they hadn't ever been validated. They had spent their whole lives listening to other people's stories. We kept thinking they needed a celebration, something that honoured what had happened to them, and to have some fun and a sense that being old was not the end, that it could in fact be the beginning.

We had heard about a women's festival in England and Australia and thought it was a wonderful idea to make older women more visible. As more women kept coming to the older women's group we eventually formed a committee. We decided we would offer women the opportunity to celebrate being older women and we would offer them rituals that honoured the process and perhaps move them from being reluctantly old to being joyously, happily, triumphantly old.

We focused on the Crone, or the Wise Woman, with the idea that in the past when you ceased to bleed you retained the wise blood and that was the symbol of wisdom. The tangata whenua recognise their old kuia are the wise women; this was an attempt to have something for Pakeha women, since to be old and Pakeha in New Zealand is to be discredited.

I think it was also a part of feeling that we have lots of things about Western society that we can be proud of. We don't have to see it as all bad and all that goes on with the tangata whenua as good. We have our own values and our own spirituality, and we need to strengthen, develop and honour it.

About 150 women came to the weekend festival that was held in 1992 at a local school. Workshops included self-defence, gardening, dance, visualisation, women's humour, women and friendship, music making, writing and one called 'Living into Magnificence'. We also had a Goddess workshop where women made their own Goddess. As the final part of Sunday afternoon we had Playback Theatre where women had the opportunity to tell their stories. We had wonderful photographs of older women and writing they had done and we had managed to create a really special space in which they felt honoured.

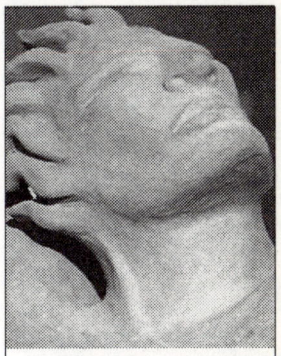

...MOVING FROM ONE STAGE OF LIFE TO ANOTHER, TO ENCOURAGE PEOPLE NOT TO FEEL THAT THEY HAD LEFT BEHIND THE BEST PART OF THEIR LIFE, BUT THAT THE BEST PART WAS STILL AHEAD OF THEM.

As part of the festival we had a cloaking ceremony to welcome women into being crones. We tried not to use this word too much because we weren't sure how the Crone and the picture of the old witch would be received. Though it is something not really to be afraid of, we wanted the Wise Woman image to be the one we were seeking to impart.

We also had a Rite of Passage workshop which was very popular. The emphasis in the ritual was on moving from one stage of life to another, to encourage people not to feel that they had left behind the best part of their life, but that the best part was still ahead of them.

Judging from feedback, the festival was very successful. One woman said to me that there were plenty of things going on in the community, so why couldn't women just do them? But a lot of women, for various reasons, especially those untouched by feminist theory, lack the courage to do things. The experience of being in a support group and going to a women's festival opens things up for them. As an offshoot of that festival we've continued to run gardening, dance, music and writing workshops.

An older women's ritual group is slowly becoming established and will be ongoing, celebrating the main rituals of the year. We have named the group Salt Water Crones; because of their life experience these women bring to rituals a huge amount of wisdom and beauty and the ability to go deeply into whatever ritual is being celebrated.

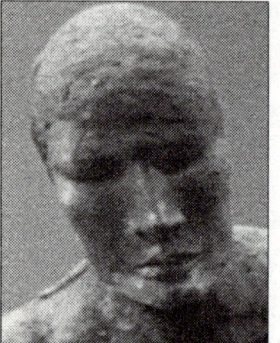

IN SOME WAYS WOMEN'S SPIRITUALITY HAS A SIMILAR PHILOSOPHY TO THAT HELD BY MAORI, SUCH AS THE WAY IT FOLLOWS THE CYCLE OF THE SEASONS...

Since then we have had annual festivals and we have tried to open new doors for older women, introducing workshops on such topics as spirituality and biculturalism.

Living in Aotearoa/New Zealand and working as a community worker as I do, I have become involved with the issue of the Treaty of Waitangi and of affirming the position in our country of Maori people as tangata whenua. I am secretary of the Tamaki Makaurau Community Workers Association, an organisation that acknowledges the Maori people as tangata whenua.

As a result of working in this organisation and staying on marae I have had the opportunity to learn about Maori culture. Consequently, as a Pakeha living here I consider that it is an important part of my life and quest to work towards the implementation of the treaty. This will ensure that the division that exists between Maori and Pakeha is healed and due honour and recognition is given to the Maori people. If we want to develop this country and the people in it to its highest potential then this issue is crucial.

In some ways women's spirituality has a similar philosophy to that held by Maori, such as the way it follows the cycle of the seasons, and it can be a stepping stone to understanding their spiritual beliefs and culture. We as Pakeha living here need to work towards a truly bicultural society and this also means learning their language. Mainly it is Maori who are bicultural, for many of them have a knowledge of both Maori and Pakeha language and customs.

We believe that we all need education on these important issues and so we have invited older Maori women to run workshops about their culture and the Treaty of Waitangi at the Older Women's Festival.

My vision is for Aotearoa to develop as a truly bicultural society. As long as the indigenous people are not honoured and recognised, we are all, Pakeha as well as Maori, spiritually bereft and we suffer accordingly.

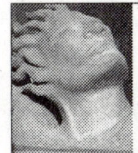

The Spiritual Journey and the Therapeutic Journey — the Experience of The Mystics

When I was working at the Little Sisters of the Poor I met a nun who was very involved with the writings and lives of the Mystics, in particular St John of the Cross and Theresa of Lisieux; and it seemed to me that we weren't talking very differently when we spoke of a sense of your own spirituality and of yourself. What the Mystics were concerned about was very similar to exploring your own reality and thus discovering what it means to be human.

I think that is where the therapeutic journey and the spiritual journey are very akin — the belief that unless you know yourself you won't know or understand anyone else. So for me the act of finding myself, which I had felt such a need to do as part of therapy, was also a spiritual quest.

This nun and I talked about therapy and that journey and about her spirituality and her journey and the two weren't very different. There was also a sense that you are your sister's and brother's keeper and yet if you can't love yourself you can't love anyone else. I think this is the big issue with women and older women: that there is something wrong with loving yourself. They are so busy giving everybody else love and support that it takes quite a step to love themselves.

So whether it is love of God or love of yourself I think the two are quite interwoven. What you are really seeking to do is communicate a sense of yourself and what you believe and have discovered to be your own truth. I think that that was what was being revealed to me about the Mystics – that they were seeking their own paths. That was a freedom I had never experienced in the Church. It doesn't need God to be up there – the Goddess or God is within you.

I've a book called *Weavers of Wisdom: Women Mystics of the Twentieth Century* which includes Marien Milner, who is what I would think of as a mystic. She is also a therapist and author who is looking at what life's about. Her quest was for understanding of what it was that made her and therefore others happy. I suppose that ties back again into the therapeutic notion of what is whole, what is the part of yourself that needs to be healed so that you can lead a life that is whole.

For me the gift of therapy was the sense of myself as a person to be honoured and loved. But sometimes you need somebody else to acknowledge this, which is what I tried to do with the older women's group. If you really listen to somebody and the story of their life you understand what has happened for them and you can honour their journey, and what made them what they are.

I think compassion is the most important ingredient you can strive to develop because with compassion comes understanding of yourself and others.

I find it hard to separate spirituality from knowledge of yourself and valuing yourself and others. Whatever the course you are taking in life, whether it is through religion or women's spirituality, I think the aim is to achieve wholeness and to develop as much potential as one possibly can, and to help other people do the same.

LEA HOLFORD

LEA HOLFORD WAS BORN IN IOWA, AMERICA AND WAS BROUGHT UP
IN QUITE A FUNDAMENTALIST CHRISTIAN CHURCH, THE VALUES OF WHICH
SUITED THE RURAL COMMUNITY LIFE BUT DID NOT WORK FOR HER
BECAUSE SHE WAS TOO NON-CONFORMIST.

She did an undergraduate degree in international relations and sociology. Her interest in other cultures and Asian religions led to a masters degree in East/West psychology and a PhD in clinical psychology.

In the early 1980s she and her husband moved to New Zealand. Lea taught women's spirituality classes at Auckland University Continuing Education for seven years and has lectured in mythologies of men's and women's spiritual paths, women's psychology and fields of transpersonal and Jungian psychology. She has also taught classes in Gaia consciousness and done rituals around this.

Lea does not see women's spirituality as necessarily gender-based or only for women. She sees it rather as a rehonouring of the feminine and rebalancing it with masculine elements. She also sees similarities between women's spirituality and current themes in eco-psychology, an emerging field which emphasises how we have lost our roots in nature, a situation which gives rise to many of the desperate behaviours in today's society. She believes that unless the feminine dimension is truly revalued, our future on the planet is bleak.

✦

I was born on a farm in Iowa in America and was raised in a fairly fundamentalist Christian church, which had in a sense a very simple, dogmatic creed. I experienced it as guilt-inducing, very damaging to self esteem and repressive of emotions.

But for my family and the milieu we lived in, it worked. There was a very strong community bonding and the values really suited the rural community life: helping each other and not being materialistic, not being power driven — none of the things that are happening in today's society. When I look back I think it did work for most of those people, but I was too non-conformist.

I'm pretty hard on Christianity and I can still be pretty scathing when I get into a feminist critique. But I do know that, intellectually, the mystical tradition is one with the traditions of all religions. Most of the time I am left cold by the symbols because of my earlier upbringing but I appreciate the deeper meaning of sacrifice and suffering for transformation.

I HAD TROUBLE FINDING TEACHERS THAT EMBODIED FOR ME WHAT I WAS LOOKING FOR: 'GROUNDED', NON TRANSCENDENT-BASED SPIRITUALITY WITH HEART.

I did an undergraduate degree in international relations and sociology. I started out being fascinated by other cultures, which is what drew me into those fields. During my time at university I became interested in Asian religions. One of the things that spurred my spiritual growth was taking LSD during hippie days; the students I took drugs with did it in a ritual context, so I'm really aware of the importance of mind-set and setting (ritual, symbols and expectations), all the power of that and altered states.

That led me into a tremendous interest in altered states of consciousness and then I became interested in Eastern religions and methods of meditation and how you could experience those states without drugs.

That led me into an interest in psychology, particularly Jungian psychology because it blended cross-cultural issues, universal archetypes and all the symbols of the unconscious which I had experienced.

It led to a powerful search early on. I took five years off and lived communally for two years, then went self-sufficient farming in Virginia. I lived alone in the mountains and experienced different models of living with people, being interdependent and independent. Finally I decided I needed to understand my spiritual path better. I'd learned a number of meditation techniques and would follow them for a while, then feel I didn't have the right attitude. I had trouble finding teachers that embodied for me what I was looking for: 'grounded', non transcendent-based spirituality with heart.

I moved to San Francisco and went to a private graduate school, the California Institute of Asian Studies, which was based on comparative religion and cross-cultural psychology – a spectacular place. I learned about different paths towards transformation and what that has to do with different kinds of personalities and the effect culture has on this. I studied symbolism and the inner world. I did a masters in East/West psychology and a PhD in clinical psychology. I had the good fortune to study with many spiritual teachers from other cultures.

Psychology was this magic, fluid field in which you could be yourself – be into all kinds of esoteric, weird things. That sounded like a good avenue since they didn't pay 'generic' priestesses much and I couldn't relate to going into any kind of religious order.

I couldn't get past the dogmas of all the spiritual paths, although I had practised quite seriously as a Buddhist for five years and I still continue to feel my spiritual teacher is a Burmese Buddhist nun who lives in San Francisco. She embodies what it means to me to be spiritual in a way no one else has.

This nun embodies unconditional love in a real way – not detached and transcendent – but through her being, her teaching and her healing work. I think Buddhism as a practice is wonderful and that's all it ever claims to be – a psychological awareness technique. I think it has its place as a powerful technique and a practical philosophy of life.

I married several years before we came to New Zealand. My husband had been in San Francisco for eight years and was becoming tired of his job and I had finished my postdoctoral work in psychology and was facing a hard time financially. A conservative mayor had just been elected in 1982. My husband, who is English, was offered a job here out of the blue and we came to get to know the country and the people. We knew we were meant to be here – it wasn't rational: time and place and energies were drawing us here.

However, as a rational reason for coming here the environment was very important. We saw it as a place with a saner lifestyle, a respect for the environment and beautiful countryside. That was important to us both. I thought I could honour my husband's background without going to

England, thinking that New Zealand was half English and half American. Although that has not in fact been my experience it was what I expected.

When I came to New Zealand I felt utterly alone and alienated. It was as if all the shadow stuff in this country was directed against America. It didn't matter what the international issue was, it was America's fault. That hurt and I wasn't sure I would survive here.

So I knew I had to find a community quickly. I was very lucky. I went to Auckland University Continuing Education just to see if, on the off chance, there was anything I could do. I mentioned things I was interested in.

Lloyd Geering had just given a seminar on women's spirituality and been challenged by feminists. It was a disaster. So Continuing Education needed a woman to do that and since I had qualifications, I was acceptable – legitimate. It was a wonderful, synchronous gift for me which enabled me to develop that course and meet a wonderful group of New Zealand women.

I have taught that class for seven years and given many other lectures in mythologies of men's and women's spiritual paths, women's psychology and fields of transpersonal and Jungian psychology, and visited other towns. Teaching women has been a large part of my life, although I set it aside a few years ago as I explored male mythology and paths of spirituality for men that were not the macho hero. I've also taught classes in Gaia consciousness and done rituals around this.

But I am aware that overall it is still the same; everything I teach is about balancing the feminine and the masculine. I teach mythology to let people experience or know that there are many different world views to choose from.

The one they are living here in this culture is just one and it is important for people to open up and find out what their heart says about it, and if they are more in tune with other world views and realities it is important to follow these. That's another way for me to honour the spiritual.

The ground level of my spirituality is ethical and I know that it is culturally based. I feel as if I structure my entire life on my spirituality; it determines what I think, how I prioritise all my activities and how I deal with all my relationships. It's the decision-making factor in everything I do and it directs me to do a lot of things I don't want to do – so I am very aware there are values which transcend my personality.

I do what I feel I must do to keep expanding my awareness of the interrelatedness of all things. It specifically means I deal with a lot of shadow stuff in my life – more than most people, I think. I try to honour people

I can't stand because I realise they are teachers and that it's my limitations that prevent me from seeing through and interrelating more harmoniously to them. This doesn't imply I handle this skilfully, however!

I'm really aware I could not have survived marriage without a spiritual perspective. It's not pleasant and not fun. It takes endless perseverance to try to find ways to honour otherness. I'm really into the idea of the mystical, the sacred marriage. It's not about marrying a person, it's about doing the spiritual work of trying to honour the other, who is so utterly threatening because they are so other.

I'm aware that if it weren't my husband the projection of threat would be on someone else: somebody at work, one of my friends; it happens all over the place. I think the closer people are to you from day to day, the intensity of the task increases.

I don't see why people would be married otherwise, it's so hard. But I see it as absolutely crucial psychological work and a deepening of awareness. If you don't do something like that and make it a spiritual priority, you just keep running on the surface all your life, running from person to person, saying 'it's them, not me'.

I was very affected by learning to meditate and being centred. And in women's spirituality the symbol of Hestia – the idea of the soul, the heart, the inner fire, of going inside and resting, and residing – is central for me. I love all symbols that have a centring motif.

I'm into all the symbols of opposites and everything about trying to bring opposites together, trying to find the creative balance and honouring the creative tension; also symbols of death and rebirth.

IF YOU DON'T DO SOMETHING LIKE THAT (*honouring otherness*) AND MAKE IT A SPIRITUAL PRIORITY, YOU JUST KEEP RUNNING ON THE SURFACE ALL YOUR LIFE, RUNNING FROM PERSON TO PERSON, SAYING 'IT'S THEM, NOT ME'.

A lot of people get frustrated with me because I emphasise the symbols of sacrifice so much. I criticise rituals that are too much fun, all nice and sugar feelings. I really think that's not what spirituality is about.

I honour celebration, but not as much as some people. I think the work is about letting go and transforming, so I focus on the dark and death and the archetype of Hecate, the witch.

I go into the dark, the fear and the pain because my experience is that transformation comes from looking at these areas of life. One returns chastened and humble with much more compassion for the frailty of humanity.

For me, women's spirituality is about the fact that half the world of humans is left out and dishonoured; not just in the broader political sense but I suppose as a psychologist I see the pain of that in individual women, the tremendous waste of potential and resources and wisdom. Once I had experienced women's spirituality and seen what it had opened up for me it became a bit of a crusade. I felt everyone needed to be exposed to this: not that it's for everybody – but what a liberating experience it is to find your Divine Self in a female image.

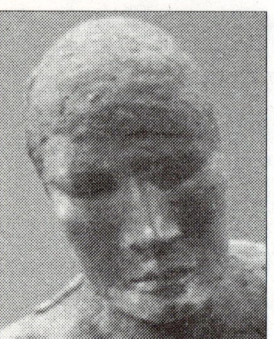

FOR ME, WOMEN'S SPIRITUALITY IS ABOUT THE FACT THAT HALF THE WORLD OF HUMANS IS LEFT OUT AND DISHONOURED, NOT JUST IN THE BROADER POLITICAL SENSE... I SEE THE PAIN OF THAT IN INDIVIDUAL WOMEN...

The spirituality movement is about liberating women's creativity in every sense of the word and honouring the body. I've felt sickened by the increase in eating disorders. I've seen hundreds and hundreds of women who are depressed and it's all unnecessary. It's not their fault, it's a cultural problem. Women's spirituality is a very powerful antidote and an equalising influence in all that for me.

The feminine dimension of life is about depending on Mother Earth and acceptance of death as part of life. Our culture demands control and perfection, independence and logic. It demeans feelings and the need to belong, suggesting these are childish and regressive.

As well as feeling that this was a way of psychological healing, it became a survival issue once I got involved in the environmental movement.

I'm fairly pessimistic about the future of the planet unless the feminine is truly honoured in both men and women.

I don't see women's spirituality as gender based, or only for women. I see it as a rehonouring of the feminine dimension and rebalancing it with some masculine elements. I'm not into being exclusive, but I feel it has to be known first and integrated before it can be balanced.

In the classes I structure things to create an atmosphere around a particular archetype of the feminine or a myth and then structure a ritual around this so people can experience going through a ritual and become more comfortable with it. I do that because it has been my own experience and because I think at first it's very foreign and hard to get out of the ego and surrender to a larger dimension of humanity.

To offer variation I work with symbols, powerful words and guided imagery and ask people to bring their own symbols of meaning so they can learn how to share these and articulate their meaning. At the beginning of each class I do a little slide show presenting images relating to the theme we are studying, because I think we are so inundated with horrible advertising images that a lot of women don't even know what the feminine looks like outside the very narrow context of our culture.

Showing pictures of the goddesses and other cultural representations of the feminine is really important to open people up to what is possible — not that it's going to be their inner representation but to realise the power and strength and dignity of the feminine as it's known in other cultures.

In my classes we study a different goddess each time, enabling the women to deal with different kinds of psychological experiences. The sequence begins with the mother/daughter relationship and the reading of the myth of Demeter and Persephone, focusing on the need for separation and reunion in psychic life. Everyone has to find their self away from the collective, to go into their own underworld, then come back and rejoin their community.

Using the images of Demeter and Persephone, the ritual emphasises cycles and season of life, the necessity of fallow periods and 'winters' as well as times of flowering and creativity.

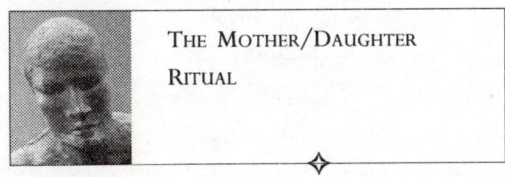

THE MOTHER/DAUGHTER RITUAL

The circle is formed by women breathing together, centring and grounding themselves. I lead a visualisation of women experiencing themselves as a tree, getting in touch with the energies that go through the legs and feet, into the earth, rooting and going deeply into the earth. The energies also go upward and branch out, and I encourage women to visualise and feel themselves reaching their arms out as branches, waving in the wind. Usually their eyes are closed so they can feel free to feel that and experience it, imagining what kind of tree they would be — who would live in the tree, how they experienced the seasons, whether they would be in a forest, alone on a hill or by a river. They are finding out what it is like to be rooted in the earth – a child of Mother Earth, truly experiencing being held as a creature of the earth.

After the circle has been formed we invoke the Goddess and name the four directions.

THE CALL TO DEMETER
(I usually ring a gong)
Demeter, goddess of growing things
Goddess of the fruitful earth
Mother and maiden
Who teaches us the mysteries of death and resurrection
Be here with us.
(Different women are at the four directions)

FIRE
Great Mother we invoke your power as Fire
Your seed must have the sun to grow
Your grain must have the fire to bake
Thus we must consciously cultivate your food
And make appropriate sacrifices.

AIR
Great Mother we invoke your power as Air
Your winds scatter the seeds to all corners
Your breath sings a lullaby of comfort
Thus we learn the ways of loving and giving

EARTH
Great Mother we invoke your power as Earth
You are the foundation, the base, the seed
You are our hunger and thirst for comfort and growth
Teach us to sacrifice for others
That we might help transform the earth into a better place

WATER
Great Mother we invoke your power as Water
Your seed is bought to fullness by the rains

Your breasts nurture us with the milk of life
Thus we depend on your abundance
And must not abuse the abundance of the earth's balance.

After that the women break into small groups; as in all the rituals, they never interrupt each other: there's an honouring and a listening.

Each woman introduces herself by naming herself: I am..., Daughter of.... This grounds them in their own experience and after that they share the personal symbols they've brought to celebrate the theme.

When everybody has shared and come back together the final ritual is a small visualisation of getting people in touch with what they want to nurture in their lives now − what they are actually ready to take care of and make a commitment to protecting and nurturing. This may be an aspiration or a dream which needs their time and energy to become reality.

Then we pass around a small pot of earth and seeds and each woman takes as many seeds as she wants to plant and nurture and we pour water over them. I grow these plants and bring them at the final session so the women can see something tangibly growing, a symbol of what they started.

In the second class we focus on Artemis, the goddess of the instinctual body, who is in touch with the seasons. We look at learning to fight for the things we believe in and the positive side of anger − how to work with it constructively and spiritually. Part of the ritual work involves facing fears of wildness, for example, personal anger or uncontrolled emotion, learning to be focused and ready for action.

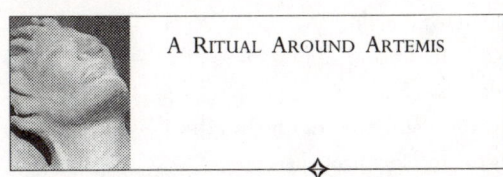

A RITUAL AROUND ARTEMIS

I start with a visualisation of women going to the wildest place they know. It may be a place known or unknown, and in their imagination they experience themselves there, feel it, smell it, sense it, find out how they feel there. Then they invite an animal to come to them; whatever it is, not to reject it, but to allow it to come to them and find out what that animal power is, then befriend it.

Next, Artemis in all her power and glory appears to them and stares them in the face and challenges them to be who they are at that moment in her presence; to see if they can stand up to that feminine power, meet it and be honoured by that power. Artemis invites them to carry the animal that has come to them and which is now their totem animal that they can carry with them always and that will help them if they need it. Some women imagine making this sacred animal small so they can take it with them, while others know they can always come back to this place and meet it again.

I invoke Artemis
Artemis, hunter, dancer, virgin
You who call us to wild places
Goddess of the untamed spirit
Be here with us
We invoke the four directions.

AIR
I invoke your spirit of Air
The eye of the hurricane
Centres the winds of the four directions
This focus finds the flow of the seasons
Just as air supports the arrow as it flies to its target
May you Artemis support our creative ideas
So we may achieve our goals.

EARTH
I invoke your spirit of Earth
The virgin forest is fresh and abundant
The baby animals reveal
The wisdom and innocence of nature's gifts
As we seek shelter and inspiration
In your wild places of solitude
May we be inspired to preserve
The sacredness of nature.

FIRE
I invoke the spirit of Fire
Your fire is a burning vision
Of what must be done alone
Your light is focused and clear

Sheltered by certainty and determination
Your energy flow touches our deepest instincts
To sacrifice that which denies life
May we be guided by your burning vision.

WATER
I invoke your spirit of Water
We find you at the crashing waterfall
The roar of the sea
We recoil at your power
But before we can go freely into the wild places
We must wash away the grime
The pollution and the plastic layers of our city selves
Please purify us with your powerful waters.

To open the circle women move into small groups and share. They name their animal, they may mention the place and get in touch a little bit with what animal power that might be, finding out how it could serve them and what instinctual power they need a little help on the side with. Do they need a raging bull (for anger), or a snake that can go to the underworld to help them see in the dark (for wisdom), or a bird that can go to great heights to have an overall vision that they lack, or a deer that's a bit flighty but highly sensitive? They begin to learn what the mystery is.

The final ritual is a visualisation where the women get in touch with what area of life they need to get focused on; they decide where they can really draw on their powers and are prepared to take a stand and fight for that — to keep focused and not get side-tracked or go off-centre.

At different times I've brought in kind of Amazon feathered headdresses and women put them on to symbolise the fact that they're powerful warrior women. Then I have a prayerstick, a sword, or sometimes a barbell and they hold onto whatever symbol feels right and think about their strength and their focus; where they are going to have to use their discrimination and how to say 'no' to certain things.

Then they name what they are prepared to bring forward in their lives. That closes the circle.

One of the interesting things with Artemis is the way she is loved and embraced by women, although a few are scared of her. What interests me especially in relation to this land is that most women only experience Artemis outdoors when they are sailing, swimming or digging in the garden.

Others find her during their menstrual period if they slow down and get in touch with their rhythms and they have come to honour this.

It has interested me to see how few women can see the instinctual power coming through the intellect. I didn't experience that as a problem with American women, because we are encouraged to express ourselves fully, the more emotionally the better.

In New Zealand I think the cultural suppression of the emotions has meant that for many women, if they are going to express themselves verbally it has to be intellectually correct. You don't make mistakes and you aren't emotional, because nobody will listen to you if you're emotional.

MANY WOMEN...
HAVE BECOME
DISEMBODIED. THEY
LIVE INTELLECTUALLY
BY NECESSITY
AND THEY GET THE
REWARDS OF SOCIETY,
BUT UNDERNEATH
THEY ARE DEPRESSED
BY IT AND LONG TO
RETURN TO THE
BODY.

✧

The idea of taking that instinctual sense of self into the workplace, the institutions, business or academia is still almost an impossible task for a lot of women. I found in my teaching and psychotherapy that the bringing together of thinking and emotions is incredibly difficult. They've been split asunder, I think because of the patriarchal emphasis on self-control; passion is considered almost a sign of weakness.

I'm very excited when women can bring Artemis forward and be a wild woman wherever they are and express that fully in words as well. I feel that's only beginning to happen here — although New Zealanders are far ahead in other areas.

A lot of women are confident in sports such as sailing and New Zealand women are ahead of American women as far as their confidence to get out in nature is concerned. Many American women have been stopped because of the terror of being raped; going out without a man is dangerous for a lot of women, so they won't do it. In that sense the pioneer women's experience has served New Zealand women's nature spirit well.

Next we go to Hestia, the goddess of the soul, the inner hearth, the centre and a ritual where women work with a candle flame. It is very simple, but powerful.The ritual looks at the cycles of Alpha and Omega, leaving home and returning home, beginning in psychic awareness and returning for meaning. It focuses on the importance of having a centre.

Then we go to Athena, the goddess of arts, education, strategy and cities, who uses intellect integrated with instinct to create complex aspects of life which require planning and self-discipline.

When I started out I didn't teach about this goddess, but every year I have included her more. I've realised that although many women in our culture have taken on the Athena archetype, in that we have had to become intellectual to survive and get self-esteem and to make it in the patriarchal culture, the cost is that many women have become disembodied. They live intellectually by necessity and they get the rewards of society, but underneath they are depressed by it and long to return to the body, so there is a split.

Women often hate Athena, even though they recognise the gifts of intelligence, delayed gratification and strategies, because it is related to the male world and the pain they experience with this world. I'm really interested in the integration of the instincts with intelligence. I hear women say that intellectual pursuits are not creative; that creativity comes out of feelings and instincts. Most women long for acknowledgement of the value of their feelings. This is where their depression lies.

Next is Hecate, the wise old woman who knows all about the seasons of life, including the necessity of death. She cannot be fooled by bravado. She represents the deeper aspects of our psyche which embody our wholeness, not just our ideal self-image.

Hecate is about going into the dark. I teach a lot about the projection of the shadow, how the things we do not like about ourselves or haven't dealt with get stuck, causing us to cut off and poison our lives. We deal with transforming those things, with letting go and transforming the energies. It's about the descent of consciousness, often entailing a lot of fear or rage. I put this goddess later in the course because I think women have to have a strong, stable sense of themselves before they can face their shadow selves. You don't just rush in; it's very dangerous territory.

We also confront ageing and how our culture hates older women; we try to begin to face how we come to hate our own bodies and what that does to us. As well, Hecate teaches us to look at our fear of death.

Women write some of their worst experiences on paper which is put in a cauldron and burnt, so that from it new 'food' for life may emerge.

The last major goddess in the course is Aphrodite, who represents the capacity to love life. I emphasise that without self-love, giving and receiving love is compromised. Rituals enable the participants to recall the gifts and expansiveness of love, as well as the severe pain that failed love brings. They meet the walls within where they have shut the doors to love. The most powerful ritual involves the 'sacred mirror' and each woman looks into the mirror to uncover the layers of self-hatred which obscure her centre of love.

Aphrodite is a real lesson in how ancient goddesses were trivialised by patriarchal takeovers. She in particular was reduced to a sex object rather than being revered as the essence of the love of life. Her early images reveal a woman of self-possession rather than later images of coy seductiveness.

I'VE BEEN VERY STRUCK WITH THE POWER OF NATURE SYMBOLS — NOT ANIMALS, BUT THE ELEMENTAL SYMBOLS SUCH AS THE SEA.

At the end I take a workshop dealing with the stages and different aspects of transformation, which involves visualisation exercises of seven levels of initiation in life.

In each group of women I find different faces of the archetype, which constantly validates for me how universal these energies are. Over the years I've learned enormously about the face of the feminine in New Zealand. I've been very struck with the power of nature symbols — not animals, but the elemental symbols such as the sea. Many New Zealand women are in touch with the sea; they know the tides and the wind, they really feel it and experience it. It's a very powerful part of their spirituality. They are also aware of the moon and its cycles.

I didn't find that in American women. They were a lot more intellectual, more involved in the abstract, conceptual, philosophical realms, where I see myself fitting in. I've found very few women have been interested in analysing issues related to the process of ritual. But because New Zealand women are so linked on the experiential level they allow their creativity to be inspired by that and they do a lot of powerful healing work with the earth.

I feel that many of the things that were purely intellectual for me about women and the earth have become real as a result of being with New Zealand women. I've loved the freshness and vitality of women's creativity here. American women are much more influenced by ideas. We're too inundated by famous people with brilliant ideas and we end up defining ourselves and our thoughts through those, endlessly debating them.

Here there is not a strong link between the feminist movement and the women's spirituality movement, although it is developing more now since people's economic plight has become so drastic.

As a clinician I can offer myth and experiences to women in their seeking for healing, but I don't push it. I am aware the educational and religious systems have been so extroverted that people perceive the answers to be all 'out there': somebody else has the power and authority.

I've found it hard to give women the possibility of their own spiritual authority without pushing it and I can't push it if their world view doesn't allow it. Women who do depth work over time can do it, but the majority of people are out of therapy as soon as they stop feeling anxious. New Zealand is an extroverted society. People often don't believe in the inner life — that answers and action come from within. The education system doesn't teach it, psychology often doesn't either and religion doesn't generally teach an inner focus. So I spend much time trying to give people an intellectual framework for taking responsibility for their own spirituality. However, it takes time for many people to integrate this into their own lives and actually live it; I think it will probably happen, but very slowly.

Unfortunately, with the devastation of the planet, we don't have much more time to change our world view so that we can live in harmony with nature. I see that many of the themes of women's spirituality — wholeness, acceptance of change and death, honouring the dark and the embodiedness of human existence — are similar to current themes in eco-psychology. Eco-psychology is an emerging field which emphasises how we have lost our rootedness in nature, which gives rise to the desperate behaviours we see in today's society. I believe that unless the feminine dimension is truly revalued, our future on the planet is bleak.

Since this interview Lea has separated from her husband.

HINEWIRANGI KOHU

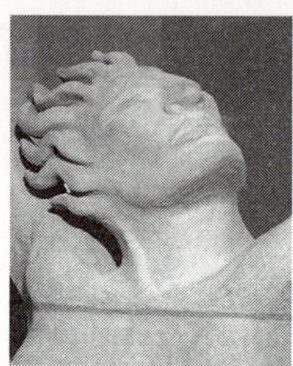

HINEWIRANGI KOHU'S FATHER WAS FROM NGAI TAMARAWAHO TAURANGA MOANA
AND HER MOTHER FROM KAHUNGUNU NGATI RONGOMAI WAHINE.
THE OLDEST OF 12 CHILDREN, SHE WAS RAISED ON HER FATHER'S
PAPAKAINGA AT HURIA MARAE.
AS A CHILD SHE WAS ALSO RAISED IN THE MORMON CHURCH.
SHE IS A POET, WRITER AND ARTIST AND HAS SPENT MANY YEARS EXPLORING AND
DEEPENING HER UNDERSTANDING OF HER OWN MAORI SPIRITUAL TRADITIONS.

Spirituality has two meanings for me. It has a colonised meaning of church
on Sunday, and having been raised a Mormon early in my life I could
never associate spirituality with just being at church on Sunday: it was
always a way of life. On another level, and the one I'm at right now, is
the spirituality of my tupuna – my ancestors, my atua – my gods, knowing very deeply that my wairua, or my spirituality, was never something
that I was sat down to be taught.

The Mormons did – they sat us down and tried to teach us that stuff.
But as a child even when I was growing up and being raised in the
Mormon church I have wild memories of a grandmother who taught me
to put my arms around a tree and understand the voice of the trees and
taught me about the wairua of everything. It wasn't only just about human
beings, or tangata, it is about the wairua in everything that lives.

Spirituality for me is about my relationship with myself and the higher
powers as such, or the atua, and because I am a woman I have a great
love and a great understanding of nga atua wahine, the women gods, who

even in Maori history have been cut down to almost nothing. Those wahine are not being talked about, but we hear in legend and story and waiata, and all the genealogical things going back to Io Matua, the supreme being, about the men.

This kind of fascinated me as a younger woman and for a long time now I've been trying to develop and get that out of the way and understand the wahine. So over the years I've formulated my relationship with the wahine atua.

Spirituality means how well I am attuned with myself and all that is alive and moving around me on a physical plane, and all that is alive and moving around me on a spiritual plane. So I see wairua in levels of understanding. As a child I see the purity of wairua; as an adult, being colonised and going through a lot of modernisation I see how spirituality has been bred out of me and something else bred into me. But now in my older adult life I'm beginning to marry these two together and understand how people believe their wairua to be. For me this is mine.

We were taught as children that we were only a speck in the great cosmos of creation, among all the atua. I don't remember seeing spirituality in an institution because unlike in European thinking in Maori tradition there's no such concept as the chapel, the church or the temple. For me as a Maori woman my temple is out there, everywhere, in urbanisation. I make my house the place of my temple, because physically this house is the refinement of Papatuanuku: everything that is in my house — from plastic to steel to wood — relates to me a refinement of the Earth Mother. So I beautify this house and it becomes a temple.

But I recognise first and foremost that my physical being is the first place and now I want to clean it and work in it — to clean it so that I become a clean, beautiful old kuia who can instruct her mokopuna.

I've had no training in institutionalised thinking, but I have been told story after story, waiata after waiata, I have been taught chant after chant in all my life from my child to my adult life. I consider that a part of living and a part of a great heritage.

The way that our people taught us when going to sleep at night, I grew up with singing a song, a really simple song: 'Moe moe, pepi e/Moe moe pepi pepi e/I roto i aku aroha/ Moe moe pepi pepi e,' — 'Sleep, baby, sleep in the arms of our love'. I went to sleep knowing that in my dream time I would have a beautiful dream. I went to sleep warm in the love of my kuia, in the love of my mother, in the love of my father, because they all sang this song.

Then, as I grew older, every day how I washed myself was a ritual between me and Hinemoana, the goddess of the water, or Papa-whenua-mea and all the wahine atua and I learned not to waste water because it was a privilege to wash myself, and even as my waste matter left my body and went into the earth I had to pay homage to that wai that took it away and cleansed it.

I didn't waste water in any way because it is a gift of the atua koha. I learned that as a child and now I only activate it as an adult when I realise that a lot of that mahi was done for me when I was very young, but it is a part of living. And so I could go through all the elements of the earth, of fire, of wind and of water and tell you as a child I remembered those different little rituals that I had to learn. And I had to learn who I was — my genealogy. So I learned all those things while I was young, but not as a conscious, 'I'm going to sit here and teach you today,' but as a part of living.

We were never taught this as knowledge to hold in our heads, but to put that knowledge into our body and for it to be part of our belief systems. So our hinengaro, our mind, had to play with it and be with it and learn it and apply it to everyday living. We never moved to the next basket of knowledge until we had done that.

It was just ordinary, all of us learned it as children. You knew why you couldn't do things, why we never went to certain places — so we practised not going there and if we did go there — well, all kinds of things happened.

When I wake up in the morning I give thanks. I have a ritual with my body just to wake it up, with all my toes and my ankles and my feet and my knees and my thighs, my vagina, my body — because my body was a koha from the atua, so I know it wasn't just from the tane, the men. A real story of te whare tangata, or my body, is simply about a whole lot of atua giving part and taking part in the creation of Hine-ahu-one. They donated different parts, for instance the kuia that sit at the 12 gates of the heavens, the marae kura, they give us a womb and the men that assist those kuia gave to us our ability to think and reason. So don't think that

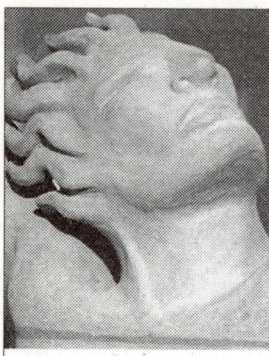

IN EVERYDAY LIFE
I WAKE IN RITUAL,
I WAKE UP GIVING
RITUAL TO MY BODY,
I PUT MUSIC ON AND
GO INTO THE WATER
OF THE SHOWER.
BUT IN THAT WATER
THERE IS CEREMONY
WITH HINEMOANA…

even though my body is big and fat that I for one instant am going to put my body down and say 'I'm fat here and fat there, I'm ugly here and I'm ugly there' – because how can I say that a koha from the atua is ugly? So it's a practice, it's a part of my being. I say 'good morning' to her as I waken, because I have to say 'good morning' to every atua that gave that part to me and every day I do that.

And what it helps me to do on a more physical and common knowledge plane is to know that this old motorbike of a body is getting old and the parts are getting older and if I don't take care those parts are going to break down, which means my life is gone and my life is ended.

And secondly I don't get up and scream at my kids to wake up, because immediately after I wake my body up I get up and put some beautiful music on. It sets me into a mode for the way I interact and communicate with my family and that's important to me.

In everyday life I wake in ritual, I wake up giving ritual to my body, I put music on and go into the water of the shower. But in that water there is ceremony with Hinemoana as I thank her for the privilege of washing my body and when I flush the waste matter in the loo from my body I give thanks that the water is taking away all of that. Then I wake my daughter and karanga to her to waken her.

After that I begin to plot the day. My day is filled with writing. My day has a balance. I start with two hours of exercise. I'm in the gym taking care of my tinana, my body, saying a prayer in the sauna, giving back the thanks in the form of burning sage in the sauna. I then come home and give myself a beautiful breakfast and give thanks to Papatuanuku and Haumiatikatika for the food and sustenance. This is an everyday, living thing. After that I put two hours into writing and give thanks for the skills and koha from the atua. Then I create.

I will fill my day for myself, I will do something for the house I live in and I will choose to take time for my daughter each day. By the time I do, I'm in full prayer for having achieved a day of balance. So my daily life is always governed by balance.

My wairua, my hinengaro, my tinana, my whanau are all part of my seeing. As I've grown I've learned many things because I have many focuses which I come from, but I don't separate those beings.

My eyes have a physical seeing, my eyes can see in a wairua way, my eyes can see into the hearts of my family and my eyes actually hear more, my ears see more and my mouth is shut more.

Looking to the future, I will walk as I talk. I know that in my future maybe there are probably at the most, if I'm lucky, a whole 20 years — I won't have enough time. So right now my major aim is to be the most beautiful, stunning old woman and the most knowledgeable and most gifted and cultural kuia for myself mainly and for my mokopuna secondly. I want to discover every part of myself, I want to understand my shadows and my darknesses and my uglies — my 'Mrs Ugly' as I call her as equally in balance with my 'Mrs Good', my 'Mrs Beautiful' and my 'Mrs Strong' and all those people too because I do understand the schizophrenic kind of feeling of myself. I like that word, it's a positive for me because there are so many parts of me — my lover self is so different to my mother self, my mother self is so different to my teacher self; there are some similarities there, but nonetheless those parts are different to my artist self. I approach them very differently, those different parts of myself, all those people who are built into me — one person.

In walking my future I want to be the best that I can be. If people should walk my path with me I'm happy to share that path, but essentially I am not looking at them, I'm looking at me.

What is my responsibility in this world? — this human world that is becoming ugly? The world itself is absolutely stunning because it's the Earth Mother. What I know is I have to heal myself first in order to heal and work with the earth, Papatuanuku. So I have to do some mahi in the different realms of the atua wahine and atua tane and bring into balance all the things that are in my life so that I will be ready to pass into the next level of life.

The most influential people in my life who have been responsible for my understanding of my wairua have been my mother and my father. My mother, a strong and powerful wahine from the tribe of Kahungunu, Ngati Rongomai Wahine, and my father from Ngai Tamarawaho Tauranga Moana.

My mother played a beautiful role raising 12 children — I'm the oldest. My mother gave me my ability to be creative, my ability to use that creativity in the best way I can, my writing and my creative ability in art and she encouraged all that in the fullest way I know.

My father, being a full-blooded Maori who lived on the papakainga — we were raised on his papakainga away from Rongomai Wahine Kahungunu — gave me my deepest sense and love of being Maori and who I am, of being true to the truth that lies inside me. Although he many times also gave me that most ugly side of me, we learned to balance what that was — now I do, I know that now. Looking back, those two people were the greatest influences in my life.

The second set of influences in my life that gave me my atua were my grandfathers and grandmothers. And there were several of those because everyone older than you was a grandpa and grandma or a nana and a pop or an aunt or an uncle – whether they were cousins or whatever. There were many grandmas and nannies that had different influences in my life. Being raised on the papakainga at Huria Marae, I was brought up with all those kuia and koroua and I learned to be with them and I loved to share with them the lessons they had for me.

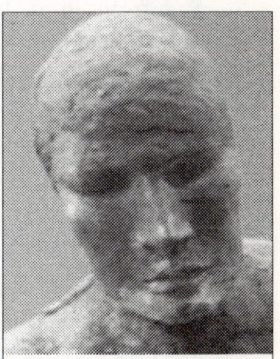

Mind you, as a child you don't know that they are lessons; only in retrospect do you realise that your daily way of life with these kuia and koroua was indeed a way of life.

The storytelling told us many of these things and my father was one of the greatest storytellers of my entire life. He was dynamic, he was alive and he used to tell us a story in series and make us go to bed because we never had TV and radio – I didn't see those till I was about 16.

But my life was full of music. My father had the strongest and most powerful vocal chords. He would stand at the end of the street or on the island – where I lived was an estuary and in the middle of the estuary was an island where we buried our dead – and he would karanga to us. We'd hear him, and he would make us karanga back. We'd stand on the opposite side and we'd call, so we learned voice projection. But you don't know those things then, you only know them now. And I learned to waiata, to sing, in that way. He'd stand at the other side of the mountain and call us and we'd have to answer him. But we had to reach a certain voice pitch to be able to understand those things.

My father taught me a love of Maori culture, waiataringa, te reo Maori, all those things that completely make up the person I am.

With my mother it was about being a woman, it was about being creative and entrepreneurial. She had a love and was a great teacher of whakapapa and genealogy. She taught me well.

My grandfather taught me of the Earth Mother and of Hinemoana, the goddess of the sea and of fishing. And my grandma taught me how to milk cows. She also taught me about beautification in whatever it was I did. Whatever I chose to do I was to do it well, extra well. She expected 110 percent effort and even if we failed, but effort-wise put in 110 percent we had won in her eyes. It wasn't about a mark, it was about trying to do our very best, even if in other people's eyes we had failed.

Then among my other aunties and uncles we had the carvers, the weavers — all those teachers, they were there. And from the religious base of Mormonism we were taught many other things and I credit a lot of my learning to the Mormon Church, although I'm not a Mormon.

I don't know that I can really talk about the spirituality in me because it's about other people giving you your mana. You don't ask for that, you don't go around saying, 'My spirituality means...' or 'My mana means...' or 'My wairua (spirit) does te mea, te mea, and so on.' Because it's like mana — people look and say, 'That one is really full of mana,' or 'That one there, her wairua is powerful.' I can never whakamana myself or whakawairua myself or whaka spirituality myself, because it's others who should recognise that in me.

So I can't talk about what is my wairua. All I know is about the development of the self and about coming and living my truth and coming out of the world of deceit that I have lived in for so many years — deceit because as a child adults didn't listen or hear me so that I got bashed for it. I've had a violent background.

My grandfather taught me of the Earth Mother and of Hinemoana, the goddess of the sea and of fishing. And my grandma taught me how to milk cows.

I don't want to romanticise the wairua, but you see the strength I have and if you think that I have it that's OK. I ask you instead what you see my wairua is and to ask other people about Hinewirangi. They can tell you about my wairua.

All I know is I'm trying to be Hinewirangi and I'm trying to honour myself and bring myself into balance with everything else.

This story might help people understand where I am at with a lot of things. It's called *The Desert Sage and the Dress*, and I wrote it not long ago.

It was a warm time to travel to Vancouver Island. I was excited as usual to go because Vancouver Island was a place I'd never been before. When I finally arrived on the island I wanted to take off my shoes and touch the papa and pay my respects to the whenua, the earth. I wondered who'd have time to meet me, but I guessed they would find me standing barefoot in the garden outside; it was the first plot of earth I saw.

I thanked Mother Earth for being there and said that I brought with me the mana of the Earth Mother in my own part of the world and I was silently saying a prayer when I heard her voice: 'You must be Hinewirangi from Aotearoa.' I turned around and there they were: three women, a Fijian woman living there and a mother and her daughter from Belau living in Hawai'i. 'Yep,' I said, 'that's me.'

We bundled the luggage into a small car and they drove me to the office of the South Pacific Forum. They said they would leave me there, go get some lunch and be back soon.

I said that would be fine. I needed the time to gather myself and be alone. I was looking through the big windows down on the street below when I noticed a tall man, whom I assumed to be Indian. He had long, plaited hair and was wearing denim jeans and jacket. He looked up and smiled at me and disappeared through the door below. Some minutes later he walked in the door. He greeted me and introduced himself as Alvin Manitopyes, a Plains Cree/Anishawbe Indian.

We talked about the pending conference, about ourselves and our peoples before the lunch came. I saw Alvin during the next few days and somehow we always managed to sit close together during sessions or attended the same sessions and even together facilitated the session on indigenous religious beliefs.

At the end of the conference we were going up-country to attend another environmental and healing conference to which we were all invited as international guests, but before we attended we were billeted out to different reservations. I was to travel with other women to Alkali Lake Reservation. It was a three-hour ride which I loved. It gave me time to look at the landscape and time to gather my thoughts about how I would interact with these people. Alkali Lake were working on a unique programme of drug and alcohol abuse and they were the shining example of Indian success. On the last night of our stay I had a powerful dream.

The dream was vivid, full of colour, full of movement. I dreamt I was walking in a desert; it was like what I had imagined the plains to look like. It went off in all directions for many miles and on the horizon were rugged mountains. The sky was panoramic, the clouds raced towards me, the rhythm and movement of the clouds danced to the beat of a drum. I felt as if I was in a bowl where I could reach out and touch the clouds as they were racing by. I looked down at my feet, which were surrounded with sage brush. The sweet smell of the sage rose in my nostrils. I was captivated by its beauty.

I knelt to talk to a sage bush, but found to my horror it was covered with thousands of ticks – the little animals that get into the skin and suck the blood. I began to panic, thinking these ticks would be all over me. I stood up and looked for a way to get off these plains because I was so afraid of the ticks, yet somehow I felt I was there to clean the ticks off the sagebrush. I looked across the plains and recognised a human form walking in the distance towards me. Within moments he was standing next to me. I was totally surprised: 'Alvin, what are you doing here?' I said. He just smiled a knowing smile: 'You know why I'm here.' He looked at me directly in the eyes and said, 'Burn the sage, Hinewirangi, put a light to it.' 'What?' I said. 'Don't be stupid.' 'Hinewirangi, burn the sage,' he said firmly.

I stood up straight, trying to ascertain where the wind was coming from. I thought if it was blowing I could stand on the right side. I didn't want to be burned. When I looked up at him he said, 'Burn the sage, Hinewirangi.' And then he was gone: I could see him at the other end of the plain. I took a match from my small waist purse and, checking the wind again, I lit the sage.

To my dismay the flames instantly engulfed me. I was burning, but somehow I wasn't hurting. As I stood in the flames, before my eyes came a lot of TV screens. In each screen was a segment of my life. One image showed that I was dishonest, not in what I was saying, but in what I didn't say. I had my truth inside, never revealing it and when asked about it I said nothing. The image burnt and another image came. The next image was one of not listening to the higher self, not listening to the promptings: the lessons I had to learn. And again the sage image burnt into the next. This image was a hard one, one I had not wanted to listen to, one that I was born to do, but held back because it was too much self-sacrifice; there was too much to learn and it would take me away. It said, 'You were given the skills of healing, so why don't you use that? You see beyond the seeing, hear beyond the hearing, but none of these things you do. Why not?'

And when I heard that lesson and faced myself, the image burnt away and another came. There was image after image after image – my whole life being exposed: not the good parts of my life, but the parts I hated to acknowledge, didn't want to know and ignored. I found myself crying, hurting and in a great deal of pain. My soul was being wrenched. I didn't know whether or not I would survive, but here I was standing taller than ever. Life-screen after life-screen, I began to see my story and I became gentle within, finally knowing what I must do – use the skills that were given to me, long before I made the choice to come to this earth.

I realised that I was a century walker with a special job to do and that I had not been doing what I should. I realised that Alvin was also a century walker who had come to heal me and remind me of my responsibility. We all have specific jobs and when we don't fulfil those, one has to go and heal the other so that the work is done. I realised lots about myself and I knew as I stood in this fire that the old skin, the old habits, were burning away to the new skin below. I saw the burning away of the old self and recognised the new but ancient self that lay beneath the old skin. I felt like a snake shedding its skin for a new one. When my lessons were finished I looked across the plains and once again saw Alvin walking towards me, smiling. He was soon at my side, smiling that wise beautiful smile, saying, 'Burn me Hine, light me also.'

Looking at him directly in the eyes I reached to touch his face and it began to burn. His life was also presented in different screens and as he acknowledged each one, it faded. I turned my back, allowing him time to discover those things he needed to discover for himself. Finally he turned around and said, 'Now you and I must clean the sage. You go that way clockwise and I the other way, criss-crossing the plains, touching each sage bush to cleanse it of the ticks, then we will meet down there.' He pointed to the horizon.

I nodded, yes, and began to do the work of cleansing the sage brush. I looked behind me and saw each sage bush I had touched standing tall and healthy and on closer examination there were no ticks.

When I reached the other end of the plains Alvin was waiting for me. He reached into his medicine bag and gave me an eagle feather, saying, 'The eagle glides high up above, looking down, and there was a time when he saw the beauty and the goodness of Mother Earth.'

He had felt the power of the creator in the winds which gave him the strength to fly at magnificent heights, seeing the sparkling raindrops become clean rivers and lakes, emptying into the great oceans. He observed his other brothers and sisters, the buffalo, moving across the plains, recognising the healthiness of the Earth Mother's children. He had seen the indigenous people striving to live in harmony and perfection with all nations of children on the earth.

He had seen colonisation and its ability to move towards destruction, killing, polluting, destroying our Mother Earth, with no care, no love, no needing to preserve. He had seen how indigenous peoples are still striving to preserve the sacredness of their ceremonies, struggling to maintain their own people, bringing them back to the sacred ways.

He sees the century walkers walking, instilling the power of the sacred back into all nations of people, for this is the sacred responsibility of the century walkers. 'The eagle sees you, Hinewirangi, as a strong and sacred woman who needs feeding also, so he gives you this sacred part of him to wear in times of ceremony, in times of personal need. Clothed within yourself, you are beautiful. He has given me the sacred responsibility of working with my people and you with yours and at times we will come together to revitalise each other.'

He then tied the feather into my hair, saying, 'This feather must never touch the earth. If it happens to fall, pray to the Creator first before you pick it up. Another thing, Hinewirangi, you must complete your sacred ceremony clothes. You will make a dress, at the top of which will be the colours of the sky, for you are a sky woman, you are Hinewirangi. In the middle will be purple, the colour of the spirit, for women are sacred in their birthing channels; and greens to browns in the skirt, representing the colours of the Earth Mother. Your feet will walk in moccasins, beaded with love with the patterns and designs of your people the Maori.

'Around your neck you will wear all that belongs to your people, and what your people hold sacred, and at your waist you will carry several of your medicine bags for the healing of your people. You will wear your own feathers as well as this eagle feather in your hair. Then you will begin doing everything you must do from this day on.' He kissed me on each side of the cheek and I awoke from the dream. The sun was beginning to rise.

I sat up in my bed and couldn't believe the intensity of the dream. I sat there for a long time until Delyse came in and enquired whether I wanted a cup of tea. She asked if I was all right, and I reassured her I was. I said, 'I had this magnificent dream − let me tell you about it.' Delyse was amazed when she heard my story.

We made our car ready to travel back to Kamloops to join the rest of the others who were at other reservations. Delyse drove and Marilyn sat in the front with her. I was happy to curl up in the back seat.

They asked me if I wanted anything along the way and I said, 'Yes', I wanted to stop along the highway somewhere safe. I would get out and pick some sage to take to the conference and perhaps if I was lucky take some home.

The hum of the car soon put me to sleep and I was woken by loud exclamations. 'Hinewirangi,' they said, 'this is the place we thought we would stop to pick the sage brush. But something is happening.' 'Stop,' I said. 'It will be a good place.' We got out of the car and noticed many people standing by a small firetruck. Some smoke was rising from the other side of the hill and we looked over to find the hillside was burning.

I had stepped onto the flat part of the hill to get some sage, when a fireman came up and said, 'Be careful! That sage has ticks on it.'

The sage burning, ticks on the sage – this can't be true! At the bottom of the hill there was the Kamloops Lake and in the distance I saw Alvin, smiling away, waiting. Even in my waking time he was still there.

I was glad to get to the conference site. I arrived at the opening ceremony, only to bump into... you know who by now. Yes – Alvin.

'Hinewirangi,' he said, 'you're just the person I need to see. You've been so much in my thoughts and last night the Creator visited in a dream and....'

'Yes, Alvin,' I said.

'Don't forget to make your dress, Hinewirangi.'

'No, Alvin.'

Here are the Maori words of 'Moe Moe' and their deeper meaning.

Pepi love/ Baby love	Dream walk the pathway
Moe moe, pepi e	of the ancestors
Moe moe, pepi pepi e	the Atua
I roto i aku aroha	Gods and Goddesses
Moe moe, pepi pepi e	from which you have
	but a short time
Sleep little one sleep	come from
the long sleep	
walk the visions of your sleep	growing still
storing the knowledge	growing up
of the dream time	dream your dreams
	and make them true

Sleep in love our love
whanau family
our love
Atua Gods and Goddesses
my love
your mother
the aroha
aloha
love
deep, ancient loving of culture,
traditions
a profound love
unknow
pulsating pain
flickering pangs
feeling newness
shy
yet wanting
of man and woman
woman loving woman
man loving man
child loving child
each
calling its own raw movement
each
touch, kiss, passion
filled with the visions
of Papatuanuku
Ranginui
in love

tenaciously clinging
to each other
even in separation
finding the way
to link, to touch
to be intimate
to reach
each

purely different
in love
of love
with love
pure forms

A global loving nation loving
    nation
with compassion
iwi loving iwi
tribe loving tribe
understanding and loving
mother earth
father sky
mother moon
father mother
forest
groves, single forest live

father mother waterfalls
lakes
streams, rivers, brooks, puddles
father mother plant life
father mother bird life
yes all forms of life

sleep little one sleep
sleep in our deep love
sleep little one sleep

Moe moe pepi e moe pepi
    pepi e
I roto i aku aroha
moe moe pepi pepi e
Tangihia pepi e
Karanga mai pepi pepi e
Korero mai nga kupu
    a oku tupuna
Tangihia pepi pepi e

Cry little one cry
Speak to me little one
Talk the words of the ancestors
Cry little one cry
I know your many cries
all different
profoundly reaching my mother

inside
speaking, crying
telling me to nourish you
asking me to love you
needing me to wash and oil
your tiny body
my mothering is full

loving cry
just to hold you close
to smell that baby smell
to lie across my breasts
body to body
flesh touching pure flesh
understanding, mother tingles
innocent, warm
breathing form
hold me
touch me caress me

Ancestor crying
dying to the ancestors
walking through the veil
separating us
intrinsically you will always
walk ancestor pathways
crying in prisms of light

Crying in beauty
of all life
speaking with the sounds

that dance in your soul
rapids
of beauty
coursing flood your tear ducts

water falls
flood fall those brown eyelids
cascading into still waters
of heart
mixing, churning, still

full you are little one
full voice
truth's voice
challenging my truth

be full throated
open me up again

A cry of knowing
just knowing

knowing what tides brought you
to this world
and with knowing
understanding
you
your role
your traditions
your culture
forming your knowledge
in the foetus
in the old
the now.

Knowing what tides guide your
    waka
Te Moana Nui a Kiwa
knowing the guides

Nga whetu
Nga hau e wha
Hineteiwaiwa
Whenua karanga
the moana
obeying that soul knowing.
Knowing your
genealogy whakapapa
Nga korero tawhito

Knowing your waiata
Karanga
understanding your
flight from your past
securing your future
knowing your
your power
use of personal power

walking beside your old ones
in a new world

Cry little one
call little one
speak little one
Cry little one Cry

Tangihia pepi e pepi e
Karanga mai pepi pepi e
Korero mai nga kupu a oku tupuna
Oku tupuna
Tangihia pepi pepi e

Noreen Penny

Noreen comes from a long line of Protestant free-thinkers.
Her maternal great-grandmother came to New Zealand with
her family in 1856 after the closure of woollen mills
near Glasgow, to join the rebel settlement of the
Free Church of Scotland.
Her maternal grandfather in Blenheim was a Methodist lay preacher.

Born in Wellington in 1932, she moved with her mother to Central Otago seven years later, after her parents divorced. She and her mother lived with her grandmother – a taciturn, Yorkshire/Scots woman – and all were staunch Methodists. After moving back to Auckland with her mother after the war Noreen married a student at the Trinity Methodist Theological College in 1951. They later worked as missionaries in Papua New Guinea for 13 years as part of the Independent Uniting Church there.

With four daughters to educate, Noreen and her husband moved back to New Zealand in 1968 and worked for a church in Ponsonby in inner-city Auckland. They moved to Rangiora near Christchurch in 1976.

Noreen, who had been reading feminist books for some years, had attended the first United Women's Conference in Auckland in 1973 and began to question 'the patriarchy and its institutions'. She also attended the 1977 Women's Convention in Christchurch and the 1979 convention in Hamilton.

After the final convention she became involved in a Christian feminist group, reading, listening to visiting speakers and organising conferences.

By early 1981, after holding a conference, a group began ritual-making and this, with changes, has since involved about 50 women.

Noreen has compiled and published a book of stories of these women: *Women's Rites, An Alternative to Patriarchal Religion*. In it she writes: 'We have realised that we have been participating in the Old Religion. This did not ever die, but was absorbed by the new religion, Christianity, in order to involve the people who still revered the Goddess. For some of us the label 'witchcraft' has been too frightening and they would not write; or they have written, but not used their real names.

'It is crucial to our way of operating that the group leadership is shared. Though it doesn't necessarily make for a better group consciousness, nor a more efficient or cohesive group, it does allow the group to be non-hierarchical. It means a ritual might sometimes be a flop, but it gives us permission to laugh at our own mistakes.

'Most of the time it produces rituals that are warm and rich and colourful. It gives us inspiration, energy and joy and allows others to illuminate our lives and expand our horizons'.

Spirituality for me means the whole of my life. It means my relationships with people, especially other women, and with the earth and the many varied parts of the earth, animals, trees and birds — everything that impinges on me.

And I think too in terms of how we are all involved with one another. This has just recently come to me because I've been reading a book about quantum physics: *The Quantum Self* by Danah Zohar. The writer makes the point that we all interact with one another, that we can't stand alone. It can't be, as Catholics used to say, that 'your religion is between you and God.' It is the opposite extreme in my view: your religion cannot be just about your relationship with some other being. It has to be about the way you operate in the world with other beings and with other people and how they impinge on you, every hour of every day. My spirituality is global and I'm still developing my belief about that.

I've always been a person with a social conscience, having been a Methodist; that's the way you're bought up. In the Methodist philosophy one's social conscience is primary in the way you operate in relation to others. My partner Helen, on the other hand, was brought up by a Catholic mother and the only thing that seemed to matter to her was the individual and the relationship with God. We have arguments about this.

My belief has always been about how you react to other people, so I relate quite well to quantum physics and its ideas.

My spirituality is primarily expressed through groups, again because of my social conscience. I have always operated within a group. In 1979, when I spoke at the final Women's Convention, Canterbury Section, I asked if there were other women who wanted to join in a group which I was at that point calling Christian Feminists.

By 1981 that group had developed further and we held a women's spirituality weekend in February of that year. As a result some of us began to talk about what kind of rituals we might be able to hold and another group decided to do more study. We of the ritual group decided we would actually plunge in and do rituals and we began at the end of April, which is Halloween in New Zealand.

So it has always been within groups that I've found my spirituality, although at the same time I feel the awareness individually, too, and in developing relationships in groups and in our rituals; also in trying to develop a philosophy behind what we are doing.

The group operates without necessarily having a leader, so the whole group becomes a fund of spiritual meaning. We've only done rituals with other women, in terms of needing to be strong and do our own thing for quite a number of years. We've been through the development of three different groups since 1981, one developing from the next. They've varied and there's been a bit of conflict in each case as to whether they would be 'open' or 'closed', with I think the majority wanting it closed, but reluctantly

YOUR RELIGION CANNOT BE JUST ABOUT YOUR RELATIONSHIP WITH SOME OTHER BEING. IT HAS TO BE ABOUT THE WAY YOU OPERATE IN THE WORLD WITH OTHER BEINGS...

agreeing to open it. One group broke up over it, five or six stayed together and three of us opened up another group. It hasn't been easy because it's been a case of organising a group, which is much more complicated than if I'd just gone away and done my own thing.

I think I express my spirituality in general conversation, in groups apart from those that are specially set up for rituals, like the older lesbians' group we go to regularly. Often the questions come up and they are interested in the answers. They wouldn't listen if we tried to sit them down and say, 'Now you can hear about our spirituality.'

We try not to criticise as a lot still go to church, but we slip in a little idea now and then; also when I meet friends and relatives, although I try not to push it too much, because they have to make their own way. Generally I am quite open about what we are doing. If they ask a question I try to explain.

In 1981 we referred to Z Budapest's books but realised that as her rituals were based on Northern Hemisphere seasons and directions we had to change these. Her language was good; she expressed herself in a way which was poetic and helpful and she said a lot of the things we wanted to say. The use of the names of Greek goddesses wasn't always easy. We also expanded into using Starhawk's ideas for rituals and writings, as well as those of *Motherwit* and *Daughters of Copperwoman*. They are Northern Hemisphere books but quite good in terms of meditations. There have been several women's spirituality diaries that had useful excerpts which have been helpful in different ways.

SO IT HAS ALWAYS BEEN WITHIN GROUPS THAT I'VE FOUND MY SPIRITUALITY, ALTHOUGH AT THE SAME TIME I FEEL THE AWARENESS INDIVIDUALLY, TOO.

No one person has been particularly influential — we've learnt mostly from books. Eventually Juliet Batten's book *Power From Within* came out in 1988. By that time we'd worked out how to change the seasons around and had begun to develop our own ideas, but we used Juliet's ideas and resources. I've got files of rituals on the eight sabbats, house blessings, baby blessings, house cleansings after a suicide, cronings, trystings and people choosing a new name.

We worked out a lot of our own rituals but we went back to Z Budapest and Starhawk and looked at what they've done. We've also used a lot of Barbara Walker's ideas. Juliet Batten's newest book, *Celebrating the Southern Seasons*, is helpful for expanding lots of ideas and for her new songs. We feel we don't have enough in the way of singing and chanting. There are some women at Takaka, the Tui women's community, who are doing a lot of singing and I'm waiting to get a copy of their songs and ideas. I've used some of the songs and chants on *The Goddess Remembered* and *The Burning Times* videos.

Very recently we had to arrange a ritual for the death of a woman who was at Z Budapest's weekend when she visited New Zealand and who was only in her forties. She had given strict instructions about the arrangements: no Christian symbols, lots of her own and others' poetry and songs, pink and purple balloons, and champagne! We rearranged the seating of the crematorium chapel and formed a circle. Later we held a women's farewell to 'our sister witch' at the Women's Centre.

Some of the places we've had rituals in have influenced me. We've gone up onto the Port Hills, down onto the beaches and along into a cave near Taylors Mistake. One woman was good at doing sculptures from things she found in the natural environment: driftwood, tall toetoe flowers, shells, stones or sticks and other materials. She often made paths leading to a central area which was built inside a circle.

The place that I live in now, Waikuku Beach, has a river, an estuary and a beach and they're some of my special places. The Ashley River and Mount Grey are influential, which makes me understand why Maori people regard rivers and mountains as important. I use the Maori names when I introduce myself and say where I come from. We live between two braided rivers on the flood plain between the Ashley River to the north and the Waimakariri River to the south. If there weren't stopbanks there the river would escape and come right over the plain. It's all-pervasive and we keep an eye on the level of the river.

I LOOK TO THE DEVELOPMENT OF A GLOBAL SPIRITUALITY WHICH WILL COME FROM WOMEN'S UNDERSTANDINGS.

I'm asking to have my ashes scattered beside the Ashley River, as the Maori don't like them in the water. I was going to have them scattered at Bannockburn, beside the Kawarau River, as I was brought up in that area, but I've recently decided I would like them scattered where I live now.

It's still an important place for me down there in Cromwell and Bannockburn, where they've made the lake by flooding the valley for the dam, although I haven't seen it yet.

I've been to visit the Mediterranean and those places have influenced me, too. I've been to Turkey and I've seen artefacts that came from Catalhuyuk that are in the museum at Ankara. We spent two weeks on Crete and have seen the excavations there. The Palace of Knossos, near the capital Iraklion, has been recreated to help tourists visualise the original. There are several other sites of goddess veneration on Crete, at Malia, Phaestos and Gournia, for instance.

Three years ago my partner and I visited Delphi and the islands of The Cyclades off the coast. We also went to Malta, which has some goddess temples that are even earlier than those on Crete. They are circular in shape and had priestesses making oracular prophesies from behind screened doorways. Turkey, Malta and Crete have the earliest 'historical' authenticated goddess sites, dating from 5000 to 1000 BC.

Our first visit overseas was to Egypt, of which I didn't have high expectations, but I've decided there're a lot of good goddess vibes in Egypt. I have taken Isis as my ritual name, because I was so surprised to find how much goddess background there is if you can ignore Ramses and all the others. All these places are important.

The future for me will be following along the lines of quantum physics, in that it will be more of a question of influences from outside, of other people on me, and my influence on other people. I look to the development of a global spirituality which will come from women's understandings. I think it will only be as we learn the way women operate intuitively and if men are prepared to operate like that we may have a hope of changing attitudes and keeping our planet alive.

I feel the book *The Gospel of the Goddess* is going to be important. It was written by a man and a woman, William Bond and Pamela Sheffield, and what they are trying to say is that women have the essence of the Goddess within them and if we don't get back to listen to the Goddess we will destroy ourselves.

MEN NEED TO BE PREPARED TO LISTEN TO WHAT WOMEN ARE SAYING ABOUT THEMSELVES AS REPRESENTING THE GODDESS AND CHANGE THEIR ATTITUDES...

Men need to be prepared to listen to what women are saying about themselves as representing the Goddess and change their attitudes so that they defer to women and accept what they say and become a different kind of person. Women too need to develop. With the feminist movement we've developed our strengths a lot. Now it's got to the point where we have to see some changes in men's attitudes and this book, *The Gospel of the Goddess*, will be a help. It's very clearly written, although a bit didactic because it's trying to make a point. At the same time it's reasoned and it's worth listening to. I'm hoping to get a few copies into the women's bookshops and other bookshops.

Before I die I hope to see some real changes. I don't think I can influence things much more as an individual. I've done as much as I can in terms of my energy levels, and the groups I've been in and what I've written. There are possibly a few other articles I might be able to write as the American-based Artemis Creations wants some of my writings to put in their quarterly journal.

I hope there will be sufficient strength in the alternative spirituality movement, whether it's women or women and men, to provide an alternative to Christianity in whatever way it can be offered – in small groups, by organisations or written publications and articles so other people will take up the baton and carry it on.

I'll continue to be in a group, helping to organise groups and talk with others about the ideas of quantum physics and about the power of the Goddess in the world and the power within the earth, so that it won't be something external – it'll be something internal within us all.

THE WORD 'WITCH' HASN'T QUITE CHANGED ENOUGH YET. I THINK THE ONLY WAY IS FOR US TO STAND UP AND SAY IT IS OUR WORD...

When we first started doing rituals we realised that we were linking into the Old Religion that had never really died, although believers in Christianity had tried to push it under. The witch-burnings were only the development of that. Christianity was being threatened by the Old Religion and some powerful Christians wanted it to die, particularly the wise, older women who were the ones carrying it on. One of the ways they did that was to use the pejorative term 'witch', labelling the women by saying they were doing evil witchcraft.

We are using the word 'witch' in the same way the African Americans used to say, 'We are Blacks and black is good,' in an effort to change its connotations. But the difficulty is that as soon as women are told they're linking into some power which is 'harmful' they shrink back. Whereas if we are able to say, 'This is our word and we'll use it,' and not be worried about all the connotations that go along with being a witch we will be able to change the perception of the word. It's a deep, deep fear that is inculcated into us through fairytales, from Snow White and all the others. In most cases the witch is the strongest in the old fairytales; she was not necessarily bad, and she could be a strong woman who had an effect on people.

Some American books now talk about witches in a funny, happy way. Because they celebrate Halloween, children enjoy witches. I've seen quite a lot of children's books that are well done, with characters saying things like, 'If I were a witch I wouldn't use a cauldron, I'd have a microwave.'

We call ourselves 'crones'. When I was 55 or 56 I had a croning and of course crone is a bad word. But I think the attitude towards it is beginning to change; likewise for 'hag' and 'spinster'. But the word 'witch' hasn't quite changed enough yet. I think the only way is for us to stand up and say it is our word and we will use it because we are strong women and we have the knowledge.

MARY HANCOCK

MARY HANCOCK GREW UP IN PALMERSTON NORTH
AND WAS RAISED IN THE METHODIST CHURCH. AS A TEENAGER
SHE BECAME A CATHOLIC. IN HER EARLY TWENTIES SHE DISCOVERED
FEMINISM WHICH ANSWERED A LOT, THOUGH NOT ALL,
OF HER QUEST FOR MEANING.

Mary has a bachelors degree and a masters degree in education, a diploma in teaching and an extensive background in education, research and teaching. She has been a celebrant and ritual-maker in Auckland for the past 15 years. In 1988 she established her own company 'Transitions' and in 1996 she began a training programme for celebrants and ritual-makers at Auckland Institute of Technology.

Ceremony, celebration and ritual have always been important in my life. The first ritual I was ever involved in was when I first menstruated, at 11 years of age. My parents said it was something to celebrate and they took me out to a concert of my choice: the Howard Morrison Quartet. Knowing that in my own life my parents marked that celebration has been very important for me, as it has given me a good feel for my own body and my own journey, my transitions.

I grew up in Palmerston North and was raised in the Methodist Church but when I was hunting around to find meaning for life as a teenager — window shopping for God — I became a Catholic. I've had lots of experience of trying to find what my spiritual path is about and I've certainly seen many models. In the decade of my twenties I let go of all that and acknowledged there didn't seem to be any spiritual dynamic in my life and that what was around felt pretty hollow.

Then I recognised we do need to have ways of celebrating life's processes and transitions and there must be ways of explaining who we are, how we are and the ways we live — not just in the ways I had been taught. So it opened me up to looking around. The Methodist perspective isn't doctrinaire; it's pretty open, so I wasn't clobbered around the head enough to make me not want to look at any particular spiritual way.

I first came into contact with more formal ritual through my feminist involvement. As I came from a very academic background, finding feminism in my early twenties answered a lot of my quest for meaning, but I felt there had to be something else. At that stage in the late seventies and the early eighties, when the Womanspirit movement in Britain and America was really blossoming, I began to be aware that a lot of feminist writing was beginning to explore spirituality, which had previously been seen as an absolute taboo.

It was at this stage that I had the feeling of coming home. As a woman with a strong feminist commitment it was as if I was finally putting all the pieces together. I really like the fact that the women's spirituality movement in the West, as a Pakeha movement, is eclectic, drawing on all the wealth of many traditions. The wonderful thing about women's spirituality is that because you are tuning into your own energy, you don't have to buy a spiritual perspective.

The Womanspirit movement is international and ancient. Every culture across time has found ways to express how we function as human beings, particularly as women, and ways to honour life. To me it's a very simple yet very beautiful form of spiritual connectedness.

I think we can use that tradition and develop our own insights now and build on what our forebears, our mothers and fathers of times gone by, have learnt and what we are learning in such an accelerated way now.

In the late seventies and early eighties, when I was in England I visited Avebury and Stonehenge and felt the resonance there. I was aware that women in England, the English equivalent of Womanspirit, were talking about traditional Goddess interpretations of places like Avebury and Stonehenge.

A friend, Peta Joyce, and I came back to New Zealand and in 1981 ran a course at the Ponsonby Women's Centre called 'Faces of the Goddess in Our Lives'. We wanted to explore our journey and share it with other women and we did it with naive simplicity.

Ritual came into my life through very simple things like the lighting of candles and taking time at the beach with the water. To me, simplicity is the beauty of ritual. It's a way of taking the very simple things of life and drawing out meaning and depth from these.

I remember 15 years ago finding time to light candles during the full moon and tuning into the seasons of the sun. I did this on my own, but when I talked about it with other friends I found that other women were beginning to think about these things too. In fact little groups of women had got together to celebrate the seasonal cycle.

So I talked with friends about having our own group and four of us for a year in 1984 celebrated the equinoxes and solstices. Books like Starhawk's *The Spiral Dance* I've found help me to see different ways of doing things I had begun to instinctively explore.

A key event for me – linking up with women exploring similar things and getting into long-term groups – was doing Lea Holford's course on the Goddess, in 1984. Lea has that wonderful gift of being in the right place at the right time. She has a real gift in that area, providing material to galvanise women.

Eleven of us who did that course decided that we would love to have an ongoing commitment to do rituals. So we formed a group called Eleven Women and were together for a couple of years. In 1986 I moved from that into Cone, an Auckland women's spirituality group, which I have been in for about 11 years. It provides me with spiritual challenge and spiritual safety because we have been together for so long we know each other very well: this has led to a deep trust and respect between the eight of us.

> TO ME, SIMPLICITY IS THE BEAUTY OF RITUAL. IT'S A WAY OF TAKING THE VERY SIMPLE THINGS OF LIFE AND DRAWING OUT MEANING AND DEPTH FROM THESE.

The group did not start out as a support basis, but was totally ritually based. However because of the bonding that comes after years of deep ritual work together, we are now a real family, acting as mentors for each other at different times. Within the group we're exploring different spiritual perspectives: the Siddha Yoga and Buddhist perspectives are quite active as well as the Wicca tradition. There is lots of fun and debate, amidst a great, tender caring which nurtures us all as we move through the journey of life.

Feminism has had a strong impact on my spirituality. It has been a powerful experience just learning to listen to the range of women's experiences. Reading journals, books and magazines from around the world which have recorded the experiences of women across cultures, ages and ethnicity has been very valuable. Some have had a profound affect.

I've loved the challenge of Z Budapest's work and women like Carol Christ, Sharlene Spretnak, Merlin Stone, Ruth Mountaingrove and Starhawk, all ordinary women like ourselves who have felt the need to share their information – not make themselves experts, just be there as knowledgeable, wise women. These are all women in their thirties to fifties who are exploring similar paths and writing similar things.

My father has played a very important role in my life. A lot of the great philosophies and psychoanalytic writing of Freud and Jung have been very influential for him and he has challenged me with a lot of material that I have taken further with a feminist and a Womanspirit perspective. Now I combine that with a more mystic approach. If people grapple with this material and debate it, it opens them up to all sorts of amazing things.

My work and teaching as a celebrant and ritual-maker link very much into my spiritual journey. In my ritual work I see my role as a facilitator, co-ordinating and providing resources. I see it as a role of empowering people to do what human beings can innately do – celebrate life's key transitions, to find our spiritual paths. I also hope my work enables people to find a peace within as they move through life's transitions.

In the Western Pakeha tradition we've lost our way somewhat. To me celebrating or making ritual is about reclaiming, reinventing and rediscovering new ways to do it. Some people will have more confidence and skill to do it than others; within a community or a family there will usually be enough resources for people to create a celebration or ritual themselves, and they can call on people like me to give added input or resources.

Today there is beginning to be a real awareness amongst a range of people who are wanting a different perspective. I get elderly people nearing death wanting to organise something for themselves and needing help to organise their funeral.

Women are increasingly wanting to do something for themselves. Since they have been at the forefront of so much change over the last 20 to 30 years it does not surprise me that they are in the forefront of reclaiming and exploring a new spirituality.

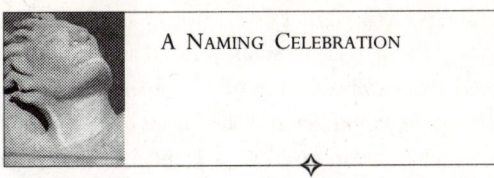

A NAMING CELEBRATION

Children's name-giving is very close to my heart because it's a wonderful celebration of life and love and spiritual connection with the earth. What I try to do is provide a chance for the couple to share their love for each other, as well as their love for the child and the reasons for the name. It's a time when people share music, poetry and readings that are close to their hearts and take time to honour loving, new life and birth.

To me, a very important part of a name-giving ceremony is the use of candles, often small candles like those for a birthday cake. Everyone — mothers, fathers, grandmothers and grandfathers, children and friends — has a chance to make a wish or a blessing for the child. It's the simplest thing, but very powerful for a group of people, most of whom have not had any experience outside a traditional church, to be given a chance to make a wish from their heart for a young child. It taps into their spiritual core. Some people may find this rather overwhelming so they make a silent wish with a candle.

When you are drawing in people who haven't experienced a ritual before you have to be careful not to use words that are intimidating, like 'ritual' or 'spirituality'. The main thing is that people are participating, so you don't need to use labels.

Often at a naming ceremony we plant a tree to honour people's connectedness with the earth and with nature. Where we can, the tree is planted over the placenta, linking in with the Maori spiritual traditions of this country, which are important too. In one case the parents decided to place the placenta in a public park, because they knew they would not always be living in the house and have access to it. They got permission from the council and had a ceremony with family and friends and planted a puriri tree over the placenta.

It's a very simple ceremony that can draw in the average New Zealander in a totally non-threatening way. People have responded by saying, 'I'd really love to have a ceremony like this to honour my fiftieth birthday,' or, 'When my mother dies I'd love to have a ceremony like that.' People are suddenly aware of the empowering nature of ceremony, rather than the traditional, ritualised ceremonies in the context of churches where many people no longer have any connection.

I did a ceremony for a couple who wanted their one-year-old named; the woman wanted the ceremony but the husband was ambivalent because he'd had a negative church experience and wanted nothing to do with spirituality. We were very gentle and careful and he finally entered into the spirit of the whole ceremony. At the end he said, 'Would you bury me when I die?' Suddenly he had recognised his own needs as a human being to have ceremony and for him the ultimate was to recognise he was going to die some time. Suddenly he knew what he would like. He had found people who he knew would honour the tradition he could not name. He didn't have words for his spiritual tradition, but he could see things that made him feel at ease.

A RITUAL

FOR A COT DEATH

I have buried quite a few children who have died cot deaths. It's been incredibly sad, yet it was a great privilege to be involved. The ceremony focuses on the child's life — a short seven or nine weeks though it may have been — looking at how the child was born and how the family looked after their little one. This helps people to be aware that though the child was with them for a limited time, through its very presence it opened them to loving.

You can have a simple ceremony; it doesn't explain why the child has died, it simply honours the passage of life. Even though it was a very short life it was about love.

The burial of a child is very powerful. You have a tiny coffin and a tiny grave and everybody physically helps the child into the ground. People can't be estranged from life and the spiritual dynamic of the earth when they are involved in a ceremony like this.

Ceremonies are empowering when people do them themselves and have someone like myself who can help them through this process. Even though people are not labelling it, it becomes by its very nature a spiritual experience because they are brought back into themselves and into the earth, into the most basic experiences of life.

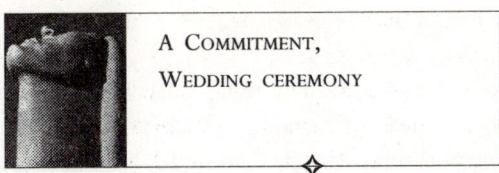

A COMMITMENT,
WEDDING CEREMONY

I took a ceremony for a couple, both in their late thirties, who had both been married before, and it was held in the garden between the two houses they each lived in. It was a profound ceremony to be involved in because they went for absolute simplicity and beauty and because they were totally honest, expressing their fullest feelings, which people don't usually do in that kind of ceremony.

We designed it between the three of us and it was full of the joys of life. At the beginning, before the couple arrived, we very simply made the space sacred and honoured the trees and the earth and the people who had gone before us. The friends and children of the couple brought the two people in.

After everyone was welcomed we passed around a cup containing the two rings they were to give each other. Everyone had time to quietly bless them. While this was being done a young man sang a contemporary love song. Then the couple turned and made their commitment to each other and crowned each other with a garland.

They had brought a beautiful silk marriage scroll, a huge wall hanging which they had designed themselves. They signed it themselves and later asked family and friends to write their blessings on it and sign it.

There are often different kinds of ceremonies during the winter, when I'm often much more involved in funerals and more inner ceremonies. As the cycle of the year turns, so the nature of the ceremonies can change.

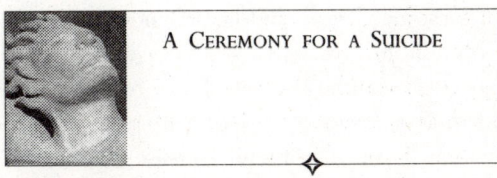

A CEREMONY FOR A SUICIDE

The two most challenging ceremonies I have ever been involved with took place around winter solstice – funerals for young people who committed suicide. Both young people, who didn't know each other, took their lives by hanging and both deaths, from the point of view of their family, were totally unexpected.

With those two families the key thing I had to do was to take time to hear their stories, to hear them talk as much as they needed to about the young man, how he lived, what he did and what he did to take his life, because people can't understand why other people take their lives.

Both families brought the bodies home after they had been embalmed so during the ceremony we were aware of telling those people's stories with them lying right there with us.

My role was to enable the story to be told of the person who had taken their life so people had some insight into why that person's journey was about taking their life because of their inner torment, not about others' lack, or things they didn't do. It's getting away from what people often have around suicide – the blame and guilt and terrible feelings of not having done enough. The essence of the ceremony is very much to enable people to see that no matter what anyone could have done for that person they made their decision which in their own cycle was right, even though it wasn't right for anyone else. In the depths of winter when someone takes their life like that there is a double poignancy because it's such a dark time.

In the first part of the ritual we wove a picture of the person's life and I chose to do that by inviting people to share stories. We made sure there was an unlimited time so people could talk if they wanted to, and share if they wanted to, with poems or verse or singing about that person's life and so we were able to thread all the different parts that make up his life. Doing that enables a tremendous lot of grief to be expressed.

I played the role of pulling the threads together so people could see there was some thread all the way through of that person's own special-ness, but also why for that person death was a more powerful option than life. Then the people could leave the ceremony feeling they understood that person's life to some degree and could understand why the taking of life was part of life, as it were.

The second part of the ritual is farewelling, recognising life has finished in this physical form and choosing a form that ritually lets people say good-bye. Song and poetry is very powerful because it can symbolically bring together images and feelings that no amount of talking can ever do.

People brought poems and music and on both occasions I invited them to light a candle to say their farewells. A candle is a powerful symbol often used in the funeral context of farewelling the spirit. It gave people a chance to come up to the casket — which in both cases had been closed, though it was open at home — and to lay a flower on the casket as well.

They were lighting a candle for their connection with the person and to honour the moving on of the soul and they placed a flower also to honour the journey they'd had with that person and the person's ongoing journey. They are all powerful symbols of recognising that many things are happening around the time of death: for the people who are left behind, for the person whose journey is continuing and for the human community that's going to carry on.

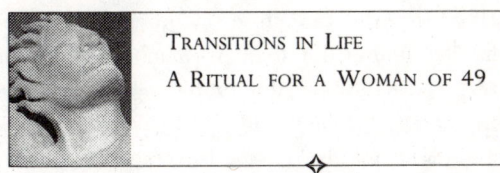

TRANSITIONS IN LIFE
A RITUAL FOR A WOMAN OF 49

The woman realised she was at the end of seven cycles of seven and was going into the next stage of life and wanted to take time to honour that.

She had a beautiful candelabra with seven candles in it, the menorah. She took time to talk about the seven major cycles in her life, from birth to seven and so on until she got to 49. She talked particularly about the cycle of midlife; so often it's seen as the crisis of limitation whereas from her perspective it was the cycle of potentiality. She recognised she was at the point of crossing over to a new stage, a new unfolding.

The woman chose to talk about what she was harvesting from all those cycles and she came out with a huge platter of big, fat, juicy grapes which were for her a symbol of this. She gave them to everyone, so they all had an opportunity to share in her harvest. Then she stood and physically passed over a line demarcating on the floor the threshold between the cycles and lit a candle which was the beginning of her next cycle of seven.

She had a huge basket of seeds and bulbs which she saw as symbols of everything which was ahead, but of which she knew nothing. She could see the seeds, but had no idea of the kind of flower, or tree or beauty that would come out of these seeds which she would plant and germinate. People were there to witness her being there, but also to share some wisdom with her of being on the next stage. They had brought little gifts which they gave her. So people's stories were woven into her ceremonial transition and it was particularly powerful to hear the older men and women's stories of rites of passage at mid-life.

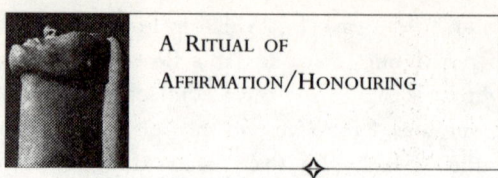

A RITUAL OF
AFFIRMATION/HONOURING

Sarah was in her mid-thirties and had experienced quite a crisis in her feelings about her femininity, her womanhood. So she chose a ceremony to explore that and created a ritual to honour and affirm certain things that she wanted to bring into her life.

She invited half a dozen of her closest women friends and asked them to bring things that symbolised for them womanhood and femininity. Sarah had made a centrepiece of universal symbols and her own personal symbols that were important to her.

We sat in a circle and quietly reflected on our own fears about affirming our femininity. Sarah invited each of us to take one or more stones from a lovely pile of stones for the fears that we had that get in the way of our fully being in our womanhood. It was all done in silence, which meant you could fully enter it without wondering, Is anyone else feeling this? You could be with your own fears. Then there was an invitation to all of us who wanted to, to cleanse and release the fear. There was a bowl we could put the stones in and cleanse them with crystal-clear water. You could see each one in the circle take real strength from being able to discard those fears and cleanse them.

There were sprigs of rosemary for our hopes around the fullness of being a woman and the blossoming of womanhood. We shared our hopes and fears and sat Sarah in the middle so she could hear everyone's story of hope, then crowned her with these, woven into a floral crown. Each person told the stories around their symbols, sharing similarities and differences, sadness and happiness.

Then we did a visualisation, drawing on the deep wells of womanspirit, enabling each of us to tune into that, visualising a beautiful, golden light of women's energy – all bathed in the beauty of this and Sarah in particular.

At the end she had chosen some very passionate and intense music that brought the energy right up and we feasted on the food we had brought along to share. It was very powerful: through this ritual Sarah had deeply affirmed her womanhood.

 A Ritual for a Child

Jack, my nine-year-old, had been saying for about two years that he would like to have a godparent. He'd asked a special friend, Ruth, and she felt it would be lovely to have a small ceremony for him. Jack was delighted to be part of a ceremony that was honouring his spirit connections with Ruth.

We gathered on Ruth's land under a giant kauri tree that had survived the cut and burn from last century and made a sacred space with the dead leaves of the tree and the fresh fronds of the ferns. Ruth explained to him why she lit the candle: to honour the north and Mahuika the goddess of fire, why there was water and shells to honour the west and Tangaroa the god of the ocean, leaves to honour the south and the earth and feathers from the seagull and the oystercatcher to honour air and the east. Jack was spellbound by the energy which made the space sacred and his eyes sparkled. Ruth invited him to light a candle for himself and you saw him take on his power as a nine-year-old.

We had a few poems and verses. Ruth read a piece from *The Prophet* about children — how we are there to raise our children as guardians, to raise and teach them as best we can but to realise they are not our possessions. She read that to me as Jack's mother. It was very affirming of our friendship and our bond in recognising that I was sharing with her a spiritual part of Jack's life. I read a piece about the lessons a child learns through positive modelling and what can happen if you provide negative examples.

We had some gifts for Jack which were symbols for him becoming aware of his spiritual growth as a nine-year-old: a crystal, a blank book for him to put in pictures and poems and things that are special to him and his relationship with Ruth and a pendant my brother carved for him from a piece of the taraire tree near where his placenta was buried on Waiheke Island — this linked in his birth experience.

We then invited Jack to dig a hole and plant the rimu — a tree he had chosen — with Ruth, as a symbol of their relationship and their bonds in the future. Then we took some time to have champagne and sparkling grape juice and food with Jack. It was delightful to see how children can fully enter into ceremony and have such deep spiritual needs met in such a simple way.

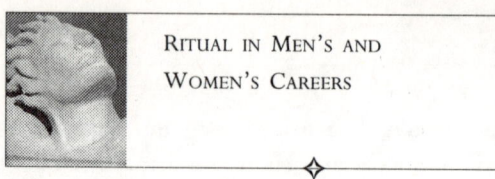

RITUAL IN MEN'S AND
WOMEN'S CAREERS

An area that is increasingly developing is the role of ritual and ceremony in career and career changes.

Anne, who was in her mid-forties, made a major career change and wanted to mark that change with a ritual and to involve her work colleagues in it.

She invited her colleagues and in the room where the ceremony was held she put her business plan, surrounding it with candles to affirm her new direction. She spoke briefly about the new move she was making in her career, of going into private practice as a nurse-practitioner, the importance of her career plan and of having her colleagues there to mark that point.

She got her colleagues to ritually move her through into her new consultation rooms and they lit candles around her work plan, too. They brought gifts and passed on some of the wisdom of what it was like to be someone setting up a new business, some of the pitfalls to avoid and some of the things to ensure success. At the end of the evening she presented them with a red rose to affirm their own success in their business moves, so it was also an affirming evening for them.

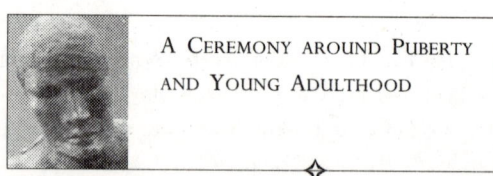

A CEREMONY AROUND PUBERTY
AND YOUNG ADULTHOOD

The mother of a 13-year-old boy wanted to have a ceremony for him and together we decided what would work in her family context. She did not want a ceremony which would involve people beyond her immediate family.

Generally, when I've had a ceremony to mark a young man's move into young adulthood, we've invited the family and men of the family and friends to bring along stories and symbols of their changes moving into manhood, to pass on to the young man.

This mother wanted a much smaller ceremony. We decided to talk in the family around the table with candles and flowers about the stages of growth everyone in the family was in, honouring the mother and father and three children as well as the stage of life the boy was at. It was a very simple, non-threatening ceremony for a family who had not previously used ritual or ceremony at all.

They invited the young man to light a candle they had in the centre for him, recognising that he was 13 and embarking on a different journey from the rest of them – a young man's journey, and one that would involve all sorts of trials and tribulations. They had some little gifts for him that might be helpful on his journey.

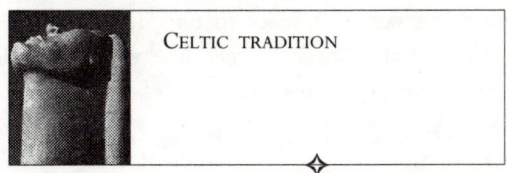

CELTIC TRADITION

The Celtic tradition is certainly part of my background. One of the things I have been discovering is that a lot of the forms we have been using, assuming they were modern forms, are in fact part of our Celtic traditions.

It is like what Rupert Sheldrake spoke about in his book, of how ideas affect the shape of society. The Celtic traditions, used for generations in Europe, are being used in New Zealand as people draw on their Celtic backgrounds. Like archetypal energy, which people who have the understanding and ability can draw from the cosmos, the energy that we in our Celtic tradition used for a long time is here now, and there are resources and books available to help us find out where a lot of the old symbols actually come from.

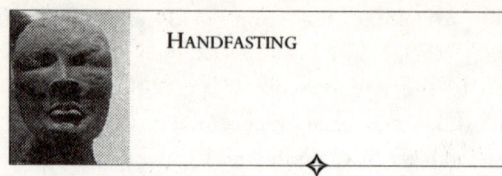

HANDFASTING

One of the most simple and basic traditions is the ancient Celtic form of union, or wedding. It is handfasting, where a man and a woman stand opposite each other and join, right hand to right hand and left hand to left, forming what we now call the infinity symbol and symbolising the lifelong union of the soul of each person. This understanding of the fundamental importance of the balance of energies also exists in the ancient Chinese tradition of the yin (the passive, receptive/female energy) and the yang (the stronger, outward/male energy).

Handfasting has been used by the Celts for thousands of years and it has only been in the last 300 years that it has been superseded by ceremonies in the Christian church. There are wonderful images carved in cemeteries and sacred spaces in Ireland, Scotland, Wales and England that show examples of couples handfasting.

Another part of the tradition is the actual tying of the hands to symbolise the bond and the untying to show that the two are a couple but they are also two separate individuals.

In handfasting a ring might have been exchanged, changing the ring from the fourth finger of the right hand to the left hand, because on both hands it goes along the meridian of the heart chakra.

The Celtic tradition is similar to that of many ancient cultures in its honouring of the earth and the four directions. I had assumed that this was part of cultural traditions which were not necessarily our own in the West, but I have found it is firmly embedded in our own background. The symbols of the animals from our north European tradition are not necessarily the same as those in Aotearoa, but recognising the spirit of the earth and the spirit of the animals is very powerful here, as it was in our Celtic traditions.

People are realising that it is possible to have a combination of the Celtic tradition within the context of Aotearoa, recognising the oak tree is important but so also is the puriri, the kauri and the rimu. Two traditions are coming together, both bringing different things. We can be fully here in this land, recognising that as Pakeha we brought with us a wealth of traditions.

At another ceremony a couple honoured the people of the land before them, remembering their own ancestors as well as those of the tangata whenua. It was no political gesture – it came from their hearts

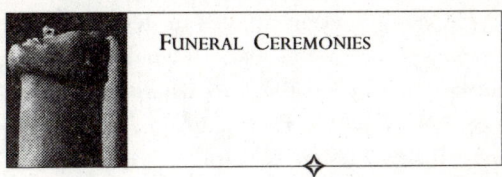

FUNERAL CEREMONIES

We can look to and embrace the Celtic tradition in England, Scotland and Ireland, where death was recognised as part of life. The body was always kept at home, where the embalming was done using oils, herbs and spices.

The women of the village laid out the body and the casket, which was made locally, was kept open so people could see the body. The family of the dead person often brought gifts containing rosemary and cloves. It was a time for people to tell stories and for children to be involved.

Local people made the pall to cover the coffin and the funeral was held in the village, with people carrying the casket and shovelling in the soil at the graveside. Then everybody went back to the home for food and drink.

Many Pakeha ceremonies today have become very sterile – sanitised – not taking into account the grieving process or the major transitions of life and death. In this area we can reclaim the healing process of ritual and ceremony.

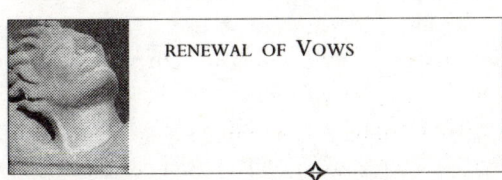

RENEWAL OF VOWS

Another ceremony I'm taking more of is for couples who have been together a very long time and want to renew their vows.

I participated in a ceremony for very close friends who had married 25 years ago in a church, with the minister as their only witness. Now they wanted to have all their family and friends and their only living parent to be a part of the full ceremony they hadn't had 25 years before.

Their teenage children were there and everybody was able to tell the stories of how they had known this couple over time and seen their relationship deepen. We waited in the couple's lounge, so that by the time the two joined us we felt bonded, knowing where they had come from and how we were connected.

The couple chose by lighting candles to denote the stages of their relationship over time. Having done that, affirming both the positive and negative experiences that had led them to where they were, they had a simple marriage ceremony within the context of the larger ceremony.

They restated their vows to each other, they exchanged rings as symbols of the vows they had made 25 years ago and I, as a marriage celebrant, declared them once again married. They played the music they had had 25 years ago – Albinoni and Paganini, then there were festivities with food and champagne and everyone danced the night away.

EMPOWERING PEOPLE

Over the last year I have established a training programme for celebrants and ritual-makers in New Zealand/Aotearoa. A part-time, two-year course at Auckland Institute of Technology (AIT), this Certificate in Celebrant Studies provides training for people who wish to become professional celebrants and/or ritual-makers. It also enables men and women who wish to be ritual-makers and celebrants in their families and communities to gain skills and expertise. The course enables them to understand life's passages and to mark them with appropriate ceremonies and celebrations.

Ritual and ceremony play key roles in my life, in my work as a celebrant, ritual-maker and teacher, and also in my own spiritual journey as I weave my way through this labyrinth of life.

RUTH TAI

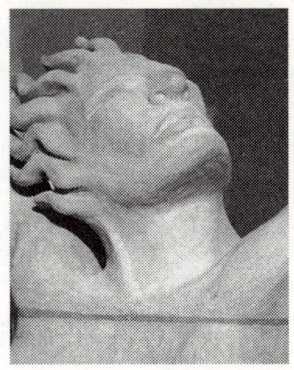

RUTH TAI SPENT THE EARLY PART OF HER CHILDHOOD
IN THE UREWERAS WITH HER FATHER'S FAMILY, WHO WERE
FROM RUATOKI AND WAIMANA, AND LATER IN WHAKATANE WITH HER
GRANDMOTHER. FROM THE AGE OF FIVE YEARS OLD SHE LIVED WITH
HER MOTHER'S FAMILY IN TE TEKO, IN THE KAWERAU AREA.
SHE WAS NURTURED WITHIN THE TRADITIONS OF HER WHANAU,
EXTENDED FAMILIES FROM THE TUHOE, WHAKATOHEA,
NGAI TE RANGI, NGATI AWA AND
TUWHARETOA (KI KAWERAU) TRIBES.

As a child she was exposed to the spiritual teachings of her ancestors, which were disguised within the activities of everyday life. Her experiences over the past 10 years or so have awakened her to the depths of these teachings. During this time she has come into direct contact with international researchers, authors and workshop presenters involved in accelerated learning, whole brain learning, human potential, quantum physics and esoteric teachings from other indigenous cultures.

The interactions have deepened her love and respect for the spiritual teachings she acquired as a child. She is now sharing this knowledge through discussions, experiential workshops and recordings in books and on tapes.

Ruth's background includes being a primary school teacher, a teacher of te reo Maori, a lecturer at teachers college, an administrator of a kohanga reo (Maori 'language nest' for preschool children) and a partner in Creative Presentations, which presented education and business work-shops and seminars using accelerated learning techniques.

I express my spirituality in every moment of my life. A while ago I went on a retreat that I'd initiated: a friend and I had decided we would do it and another friend heard so it ended up being the three of us. One of our goals was to enter silence, which I hadn't done before but had always wanted to do. So we committed ourselves to two days where we did absolutely no talking — we just communicated through silence. What I learnt was a deeper respect for words, recognising how powerful words are and that we waste them a lot. We speak too much sometimes. I found that in the silence was so much that was non-verbal, but equally or even more strong than verbal communication. That understanding was very powerful.

The other thing I learnt was realising that every moment, every activ-ity I enter into, every moment of my day, is a prayer in motion, if I want it to be. I came out of the retreat with those two challenges, feeling excit-ed. Now I look carefully at how I communicate and try to have my day be what I want it to be through allowing it to flow, through being in prayer, through being in meditation.

We were in my sister-in-law's home by the beach. We had made no agreement about how to break the silence but we all knew on that last morning what we would do. We looked at each other and walked down to the beach and it was the beach, the sound of the waves, the laughter in the waves that brought back our communication and we just frolicked at about 5 or 6 o'clock in the morning.

Where I've come to in terms of spirituality is that it's in everything I see — it's in everyone. Just acknowledging that and taking pleasure in it is something special that's evolved from my own life experience. As I move along my path of discovery and discover myself, events like that have happened which have caused me to go deeper in my understanding and communion with myself. And I can learn more at that level — the joy bubbles up more. I've gone from a very overt, overly joyous expression into a more silent expression of joy. My friend and I were talking about that and we were saying it's a more powerful experience because it bub-bles up and has more lasting power.

What I'm finding now is that even though there have been some situ-ations resulting from my past activities that I'm not happy with, that's

OK. Now, with this new level of understanding, I know that it's only a matter of time and they too will pass and the joy will be even more.

In my recollections of my early life I have always had a very strong reverence for nature. I remember times when I was a little girl lying in the paddocks at home, feeling absolutely at peace in the long grass, looking up at the clouds in the sky and I still love doing that and feeling in those moments that nature and I and everything else and the sky are one. What's happened now is that my learning as an adult has helped me to crystallise an understanding around those experiences.

I was surrounded with it at home, too. I didn't understand until the last few years just how much in terms of Maoritanga I was surrounded by the spirituality in everyday, ordinary things. Now when I look back at those ordinary occurrences I realise they were very spiritual in their essence.

Home for me when I was growing up was the Ureweras. One of the early experiences was from my Dad's family, who were from Ruatoki and Waimana. I remember we lived there for the early part of my years, then in Whakatane, where I lived with my grandmother. Then we moved across to my mother's family and most of my growing-up time was with my mother's family in Te Teko, in the Kawerau area. It was a whole playground, under the shelter of Putauaki, the mountain. I absolutely adored that mountain. I found it very difficult, when I left at the age of 17, to find there was no mountain next to me after I had had one for the best part of my life.

MY GRANDFATHERS AND GRANDMOTHERS WERE MY EARLIEST TEACHERS.

I was also in and out of hospital a lot in my early years. And I think that had a great deal to do with where I'm at now. For the first eight years of my life I spent a lot of time in hospitals in Gisborne and Whakatane because I was born with clubbed feet. I was probably one of the very first ones to be operated on, in 1952.

When I look back I realise how impactful these events were on my life. Although it was traumatic for me as a child, and I can sometimes recall the trauma of being taken away to Cook Hospital, 480 km away from home and no car, I also realise it prepared me for life now. I find it quite easy to interact with other cultures, and I'm sure it's because of my experience in hospital; my siblings don't have that same ability.

My earliest teachers were my grandparents. On my mother's side my great-grandmother — we called her Nanny Harakeke, harakeke being the flax bush — was very special. I can just remember her. When I got married she wouldn't travel in a car to our wedding; she was in her nineties but she insisted on walking. She was very strong, but quite little; a very, very powerful woman. She was a chieftainess in her own right and very assertive about her femaleness.

I remember her orchard, where we used to go to visit her. She was absolutely finicky about us not touching the fruit until they were ready. They were there for us, always an abundance of fruit, but kids being kids we'd sneak into the orchard. She'd catch us.

My grandmother on my mother's side was also a strong influence. She died when I was nine or 10. I remember her spirituality, and I also remember her doilies — she'd learned to make doilies and she made heaps of them. She had a beingness around her that was very peaceful. Whether she was or not I don't know, but that's what I recall about her — her sense of peace.

On my dad's side I had a very strong grandmother as well, after whom I was named. She features very prominently in my thoughts. My dad took me to hospital, even though it was not the tradition to do that then. The old people had methods of healing; when the bones were still very soft and not set, they broke them and massaged them and the bones started to knit and heal back into place. My grandmother knew that technique — in fact all the nannies did — but the doctors persuaded my dad to take me to hospital. The nannies were not happy about that, she in particular. As I was going through the recovery period she always massaged my toes and feet. I also remember my grandfathers; my grandfathers and grandmothers were my earliest teachers.

I loved my dad as a storyteller and a singer on the car trips that we made as a family down to the beach. I'm the oldest of 10, and I remember there were a lot of hard times. But I remember the times when Dad would tell us stories; I love storytelling and I have a very deep love for our mythology because of him.

And my mum, she's a matakite, a seer, although she has never allowed that to come to the fore because of the superstition surrounding it. She was fearful of the responsibility she felt went with seeing the 'other side' — people who had died — or events that were prophetic.

I had a very special friend in my early teaching years, called Anne Roe,

who took me under her wing. To me spirituality is a love of everything
and she had that. I learned a lot from her about the love of her garden,
her trees and her love of children. Teaching with her was a very special
time of my life.

Anne influenced my thinking about children and increased my awareness of how children learn. She showed me that in fact children are the
most wonderful teachers in the world if we allow ourselves to observe
them in that way rather than as empty vessels into which we pour information. She was a very special woman in my life and still is.

I don't see her nearly as often now though I think about her and
remember the special times we had, this Pakeha woman who was old
enough to be my mother. We worked together powerfully in the classroom, teaching and sharing. We got to the stage where we'd turn up in
the morning, we hadn't talked to each other about what we were going
to do, but we each knew how the day was going to be. Our planning was
totally intuitive.

And she was also wonderful in that in those early years I had my daughter and she was always there for me and my daughter whenever I needed someone to look after Sharene.

That alertness to children was later reinforced by another Pakeha
woman more my age: Penny Brownlie, a very special friend who lives in
Thames. Not only did she increase my awareness about how children
learned and show me that in fact we need to do very little for children
other than allow them the space to realise their potential, but she also
helped to nurture in me an awareness of nature at a deeper level. Both
she and Anne had a love for it and Penny took it further for me in that
she was very touched by our mythology, by our stories, by our tikanga
Maori. She could see within those teachings the essence and the beauty
and that was profound for me to have this Pakeha woman talking so deeply
and being so honouring of our teachings. She still remains a very special
friend.

Since meeting with Penny I have learnt to look at the whole of life in
a very different way and have begun to be more inclusive rather than
exclusive about things.

And then there was Rose Pere, whom I spent time with when I was
an itinerant teacher of Maori in Hamilton. I had a very special time with
Rose for about five years. For a long time I just sat with Rose and another friend, Pene Anita Moki; again, the two of them were old enough to
be my mothers. This is an interesting pattern for me: in my twenties

through to my early thirties I was constantly with women old enough to be my mother and they were teaching me many things. It wasn't until later that I started to interact more with people of my own age. But I had a level of wisdom which was far beyond my age because of my interaction with those women.

We used to travel around together quite a lot. Rose was wonderful, so was Anita. I couldn't speak fluent Maori at the time but these two fluent native speakers were constantly speaking te reo. I had learned it as a child but I had forgotten and then I was thrown into this. Eventually that was how I learned to speak fluently again; just by sitting and hearing it brought back the language for me.

I remember one day in particular very clearly. Anita and I were going to the marae in Huntly and on the journey I started talking to her in Maori. At the end of the journey she said, 'Kare, you haven't spoken any English!' That was the breakthrough — having had the listening time. It was wonderful, and since then it's been easy to keep conversing in Maori. Rose and Anita were always totally support-ive of me; they are very nurturing and powerful women and I have very special memories of them, although we've all moved on since then.

'PIRITAHI TE TANE KI TE WAHINE', MEANING THAT WHEN THE UNION OF THE MALE AND FEMALE WAS AT ITS BEST AN AMAZING RESULT WOULD OCCUR.

They also alerted me to depths of sharing with men that I had not observed before: to see myself as equal to any man, but more than that, not to think that just because a man was doing something, what a woman was doing was less. Neither should be trying to outdo the other. Rose and Anita would tell stories of how they witnessed the honouring of the male and female in their lives with their old people. It was wonderful to hear those sto-ries and to hear the phrases that supported the notion, like, 'Piritahi te tane ki te wahine', meaning that when the union of the male and the female was at its best an amazing result would occur. I totally believe that today and it's how I try to live my relationship with men, honouring them at the same time as I honour myself.

Then I met with Pare Kana. Pare's also very special, and we remain close friends. She is only a couple of years older than I am so it was time for me to interact with people who were my own age. We were business partners together and close friends. She came to help me in the publishing business I had set up with Rose, Anita and a whole group of us. When we established it in 1984 we were probably the first Maori women to establish a publishing organisation.

It was Anita and I who first came up with the idea. We had been teaching together as itinerant teachers of Maori, which meant we went from school to school, supporting the growth of Maori in schools, working with teachers and students. That happened for four years and at the end of that time we were told we had to go back into the classroom. That was the last place we wanted to go so we hummed and haaed and looked at all the options. Finally I said to Anita, 'All these people have been asking for our work on Maori language and we just keep photocopying the resources we've produced and sending them off. That's a real hassle. We obviously have a product that people want, so let's print the book.' We typed it all up, put the book for teaching Maori language together and printed it, although we didn't have any money. Then we got Syd Melbourne to help put the music together for us and we produced this Maori resource. Then because we had to sell it we had to do something about business. So we went to see a lawyer and he suggested setting up a company.

We did that part time, running it more like a trust than a business because we did things in the time we weren't at work. Lots of weekends were taken up making our resources ready for printing.

Along the journey I met another special woman, Karen Walmsley from Te Arawa, and Karen and I still work closely together in Hamilton. Although we weren't aware of it, she was setting up her own business at the same time as a graphic artist and her whole passion was to support the production of Maori resources. We were fated to meet. I'd heard about the Maori Businessman's Association because the field of business was new to me and I was on the lookout for anything that would help me to learn. So I turned up there one night and explained what I was doing and the chairman gave me Karen's phone number. I rang her and when I met her I saw that what she was doing was exactly what we needed, and she did all the layout work for our resources.

Since then our friendship has bloomed. She bought up a very successful business and she now runs two, at the same time as bringing up four children. She didn't want to work for anyone else because she had her children and it was time for her to put her own talents to the fore. So we attended a small business course together at the polytech and we grew together in our understanding of business.

Karen has certainly gone further in terms of expanding than I have, as a lot of her work is international. Her husband eventually left his work to come alongside her – with much trepidation to begin with. Karen is a fireball and her children are wonderful – they haven't suffered for it at all. She's managed to divide her time with them equally and also to help look after her grandmother, who had an illness.

What I really admire about Karen is that she knows what she wants and she'll put herself on the edge to have it. She's always on the edge financially because she trusts enough to know that eventually it'll come to pass. She doesn't deny herself anything.

In 1987 we ran a publishing hui, calling together Maori people who were in publishing at a time when nothing was really moving for Maori. What I learned from that is that if you want your work published there's nothing to stop you publishing it yourself – the main thing is to have somebody market it. So I've put my own material out and I've learnt a lot about marketing.

WE RAN A PUBLISHING HUI, CALLING TOGETHER MAORI PEOPLE WHO WERE IN PUBLISHING AT A TIME WHEN NOTHING WAS REALLY MOVING FOR MAORI. WHAT I LEARNED FROM THAT IS THAT IF YOU WANT YOUR WORK PUBLISHED THERE IS NOTHING TO STOP YOU FROM PUBLISHING IT YOURSELF...

Pare joined me in the business because we were teaching together. She's now a lecturer at the teachers' college, doing some very powerful work with students based on the work we had done together. Hearing some of the things she is doing makes me really excited because I know a new type of student will emerge as a result. What we tend to emphasise in our teaching is: unless your heart's in it don't do it. She challenges students on that basis, so a new level of consciousness will develop for them.

Pare and I developed a very special relationship as we set up a business together and learnt about where friendship ends and business relationships begin. But we also discovered that we had a very powerful combination as presenters in workshops. We did that for two years, touring the country, presenting workshops on accelerated learning, paralleling the research that was coming out of whole-brain learning with tikanga Maori and showing all the parallels through the archetypes and mythology, which was a lot of fun. The workshops were very popular, but that whole episode came to an end in 1982-83 as we became more and more involved with our families, Pare in Tauranga and I in Auckland.

It was obviously time for us both to move on because we were quite attached to each other. But we each had to grow in our own right and allow others access to us, rather than staying very comfortable together. A lot of our work in the workshopping involved empowering people and as individuals we can empower more people.

Pare and I went on an amazing journey, exploring things outside our culture through business and working with a man who had arrived in the country with some stunning workshops, one called 'Money and You'. I went to this workshop first and had an amazing experience at the end of it that had nothing to do with business. Because of that experience I wanted to pursue that organisation's courses; although it had a front of being a business organisation there was something very spiritual going on in an invisible way.

I CELEBRATED MYSELF FOR THE VERY FIRST TIME IN THAT MOMENT.
I SAW WHO I REALLY WAS: TOTALLY INNOCENT AND TOTALLY BEAUTIFUL.

At the end of that course, which finished at about midnight on a Sunday evening – it had gone on since Thursday evening – there was a big celebration. I arrived back in Hamilton about 2 am and my husband Wayne wasn't home. I remembered a phone call while I was at the conference that I hadn't had the chance to follow through; it hadn't been from Wayne but from my sister. So I thought the only place Wayne could be was at a tangi – someone had died. And sure enough that was just what had happened.

I went to bed feeling very euphoric; I'd never experienced that level of euphoria before. I woke up in the same mood – very, very elated. With no one to talk to and not knowing what to do with myself, I sat in front of the mirror. As I was looking I started to cry, then I saw what looked like masks lifting off. I was totally fascinated. I couldn't stop the tears. I remembered Louise Hay saying in her books that you've got to love yourself and I suddenly realised what she meant, because what I saw was who I really am. Then I realised that all those shadows that were lifting off were just that – they were other people who I had become and who I thought were my personality. Seeing all those personalities suddenly lifting off me was like having a huge weight removed and I understood a very deep level of my beingness.

I was already euphoric, but by then I was over the moon: it was total joy. And I celebrated myself for the very first time in that moment. I saw who I really was — totally innocent and totally beautiful. Since then I've pursued that learning. I now know I don't care about what goes on around me any more; my life can be in a total flap, but I know that's not the truth of life — it's part of the game of life, so I no longer worry because I've experienced a higher level of my being.

It was certainly new to me, but over the years I've come to a state where I have a lot of peace with myself at a certain level. I still get caught up in everyday things because of the people I interact with, but deep down I know there's absolutely nothing to be concerned about.

Well, that wasn't the end of that. I got up and danced around the room and down the passage and the phone rang. It was my father. He said, 'Bub, I'm coming to pick you up, we're going to a tangi.' It was my nephew who had been killed in a car accident.

My father was coming from Auckland to Hamilton so I had about an hour and a half to wait. I began to fold some clothes on the sofa and while I was folding them I started to hum. Then the hum changed - it was as if I was no longer making it, but it was making me. My whole body just dissolved; I was no longer a physical form. There was me and this universe, but I had melted into it or it had melted into me, and I just became totally one. What I realise now is that that was my sound. Each person is music in motion and for the first time I accessed my sound, my real beingness. I was in a space of total bliss. Now, when people ask me about being Maori, I say I'm Maori but I know that I'm really beyond that. Ever since then I've kept nurturing that awareness more and more.

In that state of bliss my head was no longer my head. It was part of the whole universe; it was the universe, in that it was as if I had opened up to communicating at a whole new level and I was communicating with this nephew who had died — he was calling out. I wasn't close to him. The last time we had been together was when Wayne and I had taken him on holiday when he was three — he was 14 when he died. We had had a lovely time, but since then I'd had very little to do with him.

And here I was having this conversation. He was saying, 'It's OK, Aunty, I'm happy.' And I was saying, 'Yes!' He said, 'Tell my Dad I'm OK and I'm happy.' His parents had split up and he was living with his dad. And I was thinking, No one's going to believe this!

We were conversing the whole time and when my dad turned up I thought, he'll think I'm crying about the tangi. It was funny, we were driving to Tokoroa and my dad was talking to me and there was this other voice talking to me. I said, 'Dad I can hear you but this conversation I'm having at the same time is just amazing.'

We arrived at the marae and lo and behold I was the only one that could do the karanga. It was an awesome karanga, another level again of understanding our teachings. I hadn't done the karanga before in that situation until that time, in fact I'd done it very rarely. So I let out the call and barely made it to the door before I sort of flopped; it was as if this voice was not my voice, it was an old voice of the karanga. There was a very lucid part of me that was going, 'Wow!' and another part of me was into it very, very deeply. It was a very old, ancient sound of wailing. The next thing the whole wharenui was going into the same sound, the whole room was full of people and they were all suddenly releasing from that karanga. I haven't heard that wailing since I was a little girl.

I got in there and had to steady myself and this kid was having a great time talking away in my head as I got to the coffin. I went round and told his mum who's a Pakeha and she burst into more tears. I told his grandmother and she knew — it was great because these people knew and could accept what was going on. Then I told his father and his father burst into tears, although he tried hard not to.

So I know there's more to life than what we see. While I live in this world I know there is more than this world. I have never been scared of death anyway; I know that death is just another dimension, just a transcending, not a finality of anything.

Having those experiences has taken me deeper and deeper, wanting to explore the experiences of my tupuna, because I know there is far greater wisdom than we are actually accessing. The stuff that is being put out is just so superficial; and nowhere near does it touch the depths.

My path is really searching those depths. I wrote that experience down in one of my books; since 1990 I've been writing things down — I just sit at the computer and write, then I put it away and take it out again later. Only now am I starting to put the whole process together — that's how I come to be launching my next book. From here I'll keep moving the next ones along. I think I've been through the gestation of allowing the seeds to be planted and to start growing, and now it's time for harvest.

JANET MELBOURNE

JANET MELBOURNE WAS BORN IN LEWISHAM, LONDON.
HER FAMILY EMIGRATED TO DUNEDIN WHEN SHE WAS 12 YEARS OLD.
SHE WAS RAISED AS AN ANGLICAN. AFTER 'ESCAPING' FROM DUNEDIN, SHE LIVED
IN AUCKLAND FOR 28 YEARS AND RETURNED TO DUNEDIN IN 1990
TO START HER PRACTICE.
SHE IS A NATURAL THERAPIST, A MEDICAL HERBALIST AND A NATUROPATH.
SHE DOES SOME SOFT TISSUE WORK, BOWEN THERAPY, HOLISTIC
PULSING AND MASSAGE. JANET IS ALSO A YOGA TEACHER.

Spirituality is a part of my work in that I like to get to know my clients
and see where the absences of energy flow or blocks to energy flow are
in their lives. And very often it's in an area of spirit — that passionate love
of life, that sense of being part of a greater whole, part of a dance, part
of a rhythm, part of a flow — that's missing in people. The lack of those
energies, or the lack of connection or awareness of connection with those
energies, manifests in the physical body as some form of dis-ease, lack of
comfort and lack of well-being.

My spirituality is with me all the time. It's not something that I do or
something that I practise; it's a way of being, a way of perceiving things
around me. I like to make the preparation of food a ritual; it's the connection of the mind/spirit with physical action. Being outside, being surrounded by greenery is a vital component of my spiritual expression. I
also like to practise ritual in the house, but the occasion is always more
special when it's outside.

The things that give me the greatest pleasure are those that are around me naturally. Even though sometimes one can put an enormous amount of effort and time and even money into preparing a very intricate and beautiful ritual space, there is an awesome energy about our natural environment – the beauty, the power of it – that I think is true ritual.

Without the spiritual focus and connection I become depressed. I do have cyclical depression, not to the point where medication is necessary, or even regular counselling, although I have on occasions gone to a counsellor for gestalt counselling when I've felt that everything was becoming too dark, too miserable. But generally it shifts reasonably quickly and often it's gone between one breath and the next, or sometimes between one day and the next. When I feel low I'm aware that although intellectually I can know the teachings of either Wicca or Paganism, or even yoga, which is a very special part of my spiritual expression as I am a teacher of yoga, I lose sight of the power of those things, those philosophies; then I feel really down. As they say, faith is easy when it isn't tested.

My faith has been tested quite a lot. I lost a child, an infant of six and a half weeks, about nine years ago now. At that time I was deeply immersed in yoga practice and it was my spiritual practice that brought me through with the level of acceptance and calmness that I had developed. I also had all the grief and the raging and the questioning, but at the same time underlying that was a knowledge that for him, my son, nothing had ended. I knew he had simply passed through the door and was in another room. Often when I am faced with the death of others my grief is that I cannot pass through the door and join them in the room; it is not that I wish to die, just that I wish my mission here was complete.

Tomorrow I'm travelling to Christchurch to officiate at the funeral of a friend who died suddenly three days ago. It was a great shock hearing that she had died, so I'm feeling a bit low today; just the sense of loss, of connection. The channel for spiritual energy becomes a little less clearly defined, perhaps.

Although I know that Barbara is also in the other room, that she has just moved into the next phase of her life cycle, for me the grief is that I am still here and while it's appropriate it's painful at the moment. I know this too will pass because I have a sense of knowing that this is not all there is and that divinity awaits us all.

I express my spirituality in the ritual space. In my bedroom I have an altar which is on some drawers and I always have a representative of the four elements on it. At the moment Barbara's photograph is there with candles burning around it. Usually there is a photo of my guru from my yoga training, sometimes there is a picture of the Goddess in one of her forms, sometimes a photo of my son, sometimes there is nothing. My altar will remain the same for many months or I will change it from week to week. I burn incense frequently, because for me it is a purification; when I feel the need to light incense I have a sense of purifying the space around me. I have symbols everywhere of my spiritual expression: candles all over the house, incense burners, pieces of crystal, feathers, and a Goddess-figure in the kitchen on the bench. When I look at these tokens there is a reconnection, a sense of tapping into a well-spring inside. This is what I think people need.

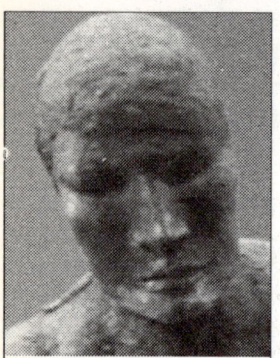

I LOSE SIGHT OF
THE POWER OF THOSE
PHILOSOPHIES; THEN I
FEEL REALLY DOWN.
AS THEY SAY,
FAITH IS EASY WHEN
IT ISN'T TESTED.

I don't think that spiritual awareness means you float around in bliss. Being on the earth, being incarnate in physical form does mean being exposed to the ups and downs, the joy and the heartbreak, the dark side and the light side. Sometimes it's just not possible to be Pollyanna. That's why I think the symbolism is so important. When you are feeling low and you light incense, although it doesn't immediately turn you into a little sunbeam, it nevertheless connects you with that sacred space somewhere deep inside. Maybe you can't clasp it totally to yourself, but you can glimpse the energy that lies there and it helps. It's kind of like the knot on the end of the string: when you come to the end of your rope, you need that knot.

My spirituality is expressed through chanting. I often sing Goddess ritual and I chant Sanskrit mantra and kirtan. A kirtan is a simple musical arrangement with repeated lines which are sung in Sanskrit. They are phrases of spiritual content and the energy (kundalini) is raised as the chant continues with rising energy. A truly amazing experience is to chant kirtan with 30 or so other enthusiasts!

Similarly, ritual chants are sung to raise energy, to bring a group of people to a focus and as a devotional technique within the ritual space. These words are simple and usually very beautiful, indicating an aspect of the Goddess, or calling on an aspect of nature which is the Pagans' recognised domain of worship. For example, the following chant is often chanted at ceremonies for the dead or at Samhain, and for the remembering of the great cycle:

Hoof and Horn, Hoof and Horn, all that dies shall be reborn.

Grass and Grain, Grass and Grain, all that's cut shall come again.

We sing this as a round and it's very powerful, very spontaneous and deeply bonding for the women who chant together.

Sometimes I dance. I like to bathe at night with candles and incense and oils in the bath; that's a very spiritual experience for me. When I take off my clothes and climb into the hot water and sink into the scent and the steam, there is a feeling of release and surrender. I have difficulty with release and surrender, most of the time. I tend to be very much in control in my life. I think it's important for women who have to be in control to learn to surrender even if it's just to the caress of a hot bath.

At the moment I don't have a partner but I like to think that a partnership could also be an expression of spirituality. I'm sure for many women that it is, because they share their spirituality with their partner and while it's not essential for my partner to believe as I do, it is essential that they be aware of their spirituality. I don't think I could spend a lot of time, my life, with somebody who was unaware of themselves as a spiritual being primarily. For me, I think the spiritual level of my being is the most vital.

My women friends are very powerful influences on my spirituality. I find that women talk about spirituality with great ease. Men talk about it with much greater difficulty, though this is a generalisation of course and I'm prone to generalisations. At

HOOF AND HORN,
HOOF AND HORN,
ALL THAT DIES
SHALL BE REBORN.

GRASS AND GRAIN,
GRASS AND GRAIN,
ALL THAT'S CUT
SHALL COME AGAIN.

the Satyananda Ashram where I spent many happy years — non-residential for me — I became close friends with many of the swamis, who were committed to a devotional life of yogic training, and were in residence. I have observed that the males tended, when talking about the teachings of their own processes, to be very objective. They would quote from the sutras or writing of Patanjali (an ancient Indian wise man whose teachings are used as basic texts for several kinds of yoga) or they would give specific examples of observations they had made. It was almost the spiritual path reduced to an academic or perhaps intellectual mode.

The women, on the other hand, although they were immersed in the yoga just as much as the males, shared their personal experiences in a far more subjective way; they allowed emotion and spirit to be at the forefront of their speech and their sharing. The men were much more reserved, almost removed from the personal within their experience. I read somewhere once that women use 'gossip' as a way of networking. On any level, I think this is a great gift to the females of the race, and men should learn to gossip, too.

The death of my son was a huge influence, so I would have to list him amongst the people who have influenced me strongly. The manner of his death was gentle, yet at the same time quite relentlessly, remorselessly draining. I spent all my time with him and I meditated a great deal with my eyes open and with him as the focus of my meditation. I felt a bonding and a connection with him that was very strong and I know the way that I felt then, although it was difficult and harsh, was an altered state of reality for most of the time. There was a sense that this would be a good way to be, a good way to live my life, with one eye on the infinite and one eye looking where my feet were going.

My women friends are still the well-head for me. When I'm low, when I'm irritated, when I need to reach out and make a connection with somebody, it's a woman I reach for. Sometimes we just talk about issues that are affecting our society today. There's such a paradigm shift happening in the consciousness of the human race at the moment; it's hard not to become enthusiastic when you are talking about the evolution of humankind. We do quite a lot of that, too, and that's an inspiration.

At present we are experiencing a shift in the pattern of human consciousness: a huge leap that we are in the process of making as a species. For many years — centuries — our race has been in a dark time where the focus has been on material expansion, power struggles, boundary disputes, separation and war. This is the Iron Age, the age of fear and confusion — 'the dark night of the soul'. We are just coming out of the age of Pisces, an age of individualism, separation of consciousness and self-motivation, and are moving towards the age of Aquarius, which takes over during the next 30 years, increasing in effect all the time. The human race now looks towards group consciousness and the health of the international or planetary spirit/mind. Times are tough and there is much upheaval, which is part of the cleansing process we are going through in order to settle into the new way. Some will not make the change; they will become afraid and shrink back, settling for the known and the familiar, too scared to open to the new energies and they will lose impetus in their movement towards new consciousness. That's why it is so important that we run with the sense of expansion, that we dare to fly.

Thousands of people are, of course, open to these new perceptions of how to live together and to the new consciousness; hence the emergence of books like the The Celestine Prophesy, which was written for the mainstreamer and is not too intellectual or highbrow, but contains good and interesting material. The Aquarian Conspiracy that came out in the 1980s is another good book that pointed in this new direction. The new age is the movement of energy; of course it is not really 'new', but it is a way of seeing/being for most of us. Also, there are many great teachers that have chosen to incarnate at this time as guides for the race in this our crossover. We have so much happening at the moment. Channelled information is coming from incorporeal entities, all saying the same thing, or similar: now is the time, trust the process, open your heart and take a leap into the unknown.

My mother and I talk sometimes and she is an influence, albeit a less direct one. I'm one of those people who spend a lot of time in their head. I think a lot – too much, perhaps – and practising a meditation, whether it's a waking, walking, working meditation, or a still, internalised meditation, is a vital means for me to remain healthy and well. I don't know how people survive without a sense of spirit.

There is a piece of land south of Auckland, north of Hamilton, where there was an ashram I trained on and that was very influential for me. You could feel the energy of the land. At 4.30 in the morning when we got up to go to yoga practice in the Saddhana room it was very cold sometimes and the stars were clear and close in the sky – almost in reach, it looked like.

Water is influential, as is the untouched land. I find that church is, too – any place where people have gathered and raised energy through prayer or singing. Whatever their belief, whether they call themselves Christians or Pagans or Muslims, it's all energy to me, and the place they practise in or worship in absorbs the energy and becomes a place of power. Tops of hills, too: I used to live near a hill called the Harbour Cone, and that hill and my garden at the foot of the hill were very special places for me. It's been really hard for me because I've moved into a suburb in town in order to practise from home and so that life can be easier for managing my son, who's eight. That means I no longer have my beautiful garden with all the trees and a Harbour Cone towering above us, the fields around us and the bush. Instead I have a small garden surrounded by fences and walls and neighbours. It feels a bit like a suburban desert. I have planted things but they are still small and I need very soon to go to the bush or to the hills and the sea.

My bedroom is a very special place. I have a high need for space, personal space, for privacy. Even when I was in my last relationship some years ago I needed a room of my own and I think that would always be a requirement. I don't think I could handle not having my own room again. In part I think that comes from childhood, when I didn't have my own room, but it also comes from the quiet space I like to be in. And from being a single parent: when there's just two of you it becomes intense. Before I was a single parent of Joshua I was a single parent of Gareth and Shannon, so I've been single-parenting for the last 12 years and the need for space can become intense. My room always has the tools of the ritual woman's trade — an altar and my precious things.

THE NEW AGE IS THE MOVEMENT OF ENERGY; OF COURSE, IT IS NOT REALLY 'NEW', BUT IT IS A WAY OF SEEING/BEING FOR MOST OF US.

The circle I was in was a Diannic circle. We worshipped only the Goddess, we celebrated only Goddess energy and I think that might have been why I left: I don't believe in extremes. As a naturopath I am not extreme, I believe in balance. And while my primary deity is Goddess, I don't believe that the human mind can comprehend what comes after here. I believe there's light and I know I'll go there, that's all I really know. I think that deity is all-encompassing; it is not male or female, it is not human-shaped, it is beyond comprehension, it is everything, all.

I don't think I could ever embrace the Christian faith again. I was raised as an Anglican, but their interpretation of God didn't do a lot for me. My spirituality unfolds, it changes all the time. So while I still practise ritual and join the women at the sabbats and I will still sing to the Goddess, I no longer have an aversion to prayers using the name 'God'. I just allow the word to be there, while my knowing is that God, Goddess, All There Is, is not male or female.

I hope for it in the future and I do feel the increasing sense of wholeness to my spirituality. It's becoming more and more a part of me, an expression of me. It's a process that's unfolding, becoming deeper, stronger and wider. I can't hurry the process, I don't even need to hurry the process, I know it's there and I know it's unfolding and I'm in the centre of it. It comes from me and it also creates me in the way I am.

I will always perform ritual because I believe human beings express themselves through ritual, define themselves by their rituals, reassure themselves in their rituals.

I like to think that I soften as I grow old and my spirituality becomes more me than my physicality and that perhaps that's how we make the transition in the fullness of our time — we become less physical and more spiritual. The answer to the woes and illnesses and sadness and pain of the human species is spirit. It's only through seeking the spirit, finding spirit and becoming spirit that we can survive the things we have created for ourselves.

Often we need to go through hardship or a steep learning curve as a sort of purification by fire in order to learn, because without our spirituality we are nothing. Every person I know who has suffered pain and loss or difficulty or great trauma in their life has come through it unscathed because of their spirituality and that's been my experience, too. I hear always the voices, soft and quiet, but with me all the time, reassuring me. I know there is guidance; we only have to ask to be shown and we are. And when human beings accept guidance they'll stop fucking up the planet and we'll be less full of fear, less territorial and less hungry.

I believe that all that dies is reborn, again and again, and that in each lifetime we learn. This is the essence of my spirituality: that I can learn, I can grow and ascend into the light to be renewed, to come here and play again and learn and grow.

CATHIE DUNSFORD

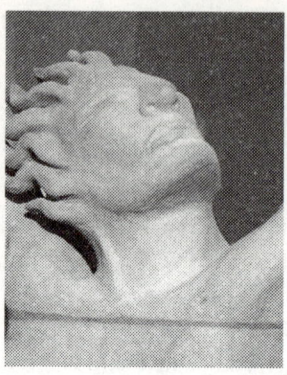

CATHIE DUNSFORD WAS BORN IN AUCKLAND ON THE SLOPES OF
NORTH HEAD, IN THE SHADE OF RANGITOTO AND BESIDE THE
SINGING WATERS OF THE WAITEMATA.
SHE GREW UP BETWEEN RANGITOTO AND LAKE PUPUKE, THE WATERY
CRATER FORMED FROM THE ERUPTION OF RANGITOTO, IN THE
CITY OF VOLCANOES, WITH FREQUENT TRIPS TO HER
ANCESTRAL SPIRIT LAND OF THE HOKIANGA, TAI TOKERAU,
WHERE MUCH OF HER FICTION IS SET.

She was raised to appreciate all forms of spirituality, beginning with a love of stories from the Bible and Pacific mythology through to embracing Buddhism in her teens and a passion for the magnificent music of the church which she felt held its true spirit. She later became interested in the Ratana Church and the Baha'i faith, then feminist spirituality.

She finally embraced her spirituality in the process of living and working with her ideals by creating a career that reflected all her deep spiritual beliefs and by supporting other writers to help them achieve their own fulfilment through their creativity. She now feels her spirituality is reflected in her novels, poetry and her work with writers, and in the lifestyle she has created at her retreat, Mohala, on the Tawharanui Peninsula north of Auckland.

Cathie Dunsford currently teaches writing and publishing at Auckland University and helps writers prepare their work and bring it into print through Dunsford Publishing Consultants. This is a lifelong dream reflecting a merging of the spiritual and political as complementary rather than opposing energies.

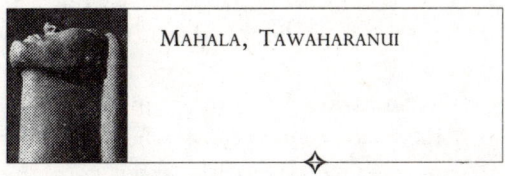

MAHALA, TAWAHARANUI

The cool green of the trees and the ancient mamaku ferns create a secluded environment. The sea, blue and peaceful, is at the end of a native bush pathway.

My spirituality is here, nature is my church, my spirituality, particularly the nature of Aotearoa. It's from this resting place, this retreat, that I can move out into the world and express my spirituality with others and for me it's through my work.

It's taken a long time in my life to find the work I really want to be doing. I've always been engaged in artistic work, work to do with words and literature or images, and I've explored a lot of areas of that. But working with my publishing consultancy and finding work that totally expresses what I want spiritually has been an absolute joy to me. It means there is a match between what I do in the world and my spiritual beliefs. I find it quite disturbing to find movements or people whom I consider to be very spiritual who then indulge in abusive behaviour. There has to be a mixture of the political and spiritual for it to work. We are how we act, towards ourselves and towards others.

To me spirituality is where both connect, where the thought patterns, desires, rituals – whatever work you are doing – actually match. So it's the integrity of combining the outer and inner world for me that is important.

I apply that in work terms when each manuscript comes in. I don't just look at it as a professional publishing consultant and in the way an editor in a publishing house would look at it: is this going to be commercial for us? I look at each piece of work as somebody's spiritual whole. It might be pain, it might be joy, it could be any range of emotions or motivations that has brought the author to the place of writing that book.

It doesn't matter to me whether the book comes in a form which is immediately publishable or not, because I don't think that is the question. The important question to ask is, 'Who is the person, why did they write the book? What do they want to do with this work?' Some people don't want to publish, some want to share things, some want to share things with their grandchildren. I see every manuscript as a journey and it's my job as a publishing consultant — and I perceive it as a very spiritual role in the way I enact it — to help that person find why they've gone on that journey, why they've written the book, what it means to them and therefore what they want to do with it.

I SEE A DISLOCATION BETWEEN THE WAY SOME IN THE PROFESSIONAL WORLD, THE OUTER WORLD — THE NON-SPIRITUAL WORLD — SEE WRITING AND THE WAY I LOOK AT IT.

So I take each manuscript on its own terms. I think there are some people who want to write to make money, for whom it's largely a commercial proposition; but most people who write want to express something. There is something deeper going on within them. Also, I think you've got to have respect for someone who gets a manuscript to that stage, because you know that years have gone into it. And that's where I see a real dislocation between the way some in the professional world, the outer world — the non-spiritual world — see writing and the way I look at it.

Another area of spirituality is in my own personal relationships and the way I conduct my life. I like to try to match that inner integrity with what I'm doing on the outside. I used to be a person who was always out there in the world, like so many other creative people, with enormous energy for everything and everyone. I've come in the last decade to live amidst nature, beside the ocean, which allows me the meditative time I need and this affects the quality time I put into a manuscript. If I'm at a publishing house working on a manuscript there are people around, there are interruptions; you cannot give your whole to it. Here, I don't eat during the day. I get up in the morning, work on the manuscript all day, sleep on it at night and let the subconscious work on the text also. That way you've got total focus to concentrate on the manuscript.

Thinking about expressing spirituality on all levels that there are, is about taking quality time. I think you have to take time to reconnect with yourself and see that what you started last year seemed to be in line with your beliefs, but maybe it's gone slightly off track, or in other directions — or somehow you've got really hyper, drinking too much coffee. It's easy to go back into what I call the other world. For me it's a process of checking in again. A lot of people work well in an urban environment, but I find I need to be with the trees and I need to be near the ocean; I absolutely have to be. When I was in America on the Fulbright scholarship I was often at conferences inside the heart of America, miles away from the ocean and I literally felt a physical withdrawal. I found that very difficult. That's the result of being born in Aotearoa, for all of us — Maori, Pakeha, anybody born here who connects with the spirit. I don't think you can go more than 80 kilometres from the sea. There's an amazing sort of pull that the sea has.

Obviously, as Jung said, there are many images of the subconscious to do with the sea. I notice these particularly in women's writings — images of submersion, the nourishment the ocean can give you and also the fact it can drown you if you are not careful. I explored this on literal and mythological levels in my novel *Cowrie.*

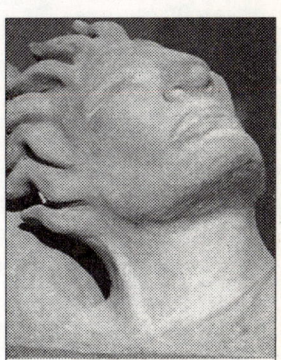

I don't see expressing spirituality as a theory or an intellectual idea outside of myself. I see it totally connected with who I am and how I function in the world. That doesn't mean to say I'm perfect or that it's always in synch; it's the process that's exciting. For the first 30 years of my life I've been acting as a medium to get other people's creativity out in the world, whether that was through my work in university courses or through creative writing courses.

I'VE USED DREAMS A LOT, BASING WORKSHOPS AROUND ACCESSING DREAMS THROUGH WRITING.

I ran what we think is the country's first multicultural marae called Te Kotahitanga for the city council in Whangarei. There we had Vietnamese people, Maori people, Samoan people — everyone had a chance to host other groups on that marae. I believe in biculturalism but I strongly believe that multiculturalism has to happen at the same time. And I don't see there's a hierarchy. Obviously this country must work essentially in partnership but we must also move out beyond that and build on it. My work as literary director of the first Sing Aotearoa Festival was based on that partnership model.

At a personal level *Cowrie,* the novel, is my spirituality out in the world. It's taken 40 years for me to allow myself the time and the indulgence to express publicly my own creativity and spirituality.

There have been some amazing reactions to *Cowrie*. A British critic who interviewed me for 2SER FM Sydney had given it to a friend of hers who read it on the shores of a lake in Malawi. She wrote me this incredible letter and said her friend read the book between swimming in the lake and it was like being inside a dream. She didn't want it to end. An Australian woman said it reinforced her belief in humanity and the power of love which she had lost. Another woman from Internal Affairs in Wellington who is really intellectual said she had to lie down and dream as she was reading it. So there was this whole process going on. That's precisely what I wanted to happen. And the turtle mythology and everything that went with it — I wanted people to be drawn into it.

Cowrie was partly based on my own background and exploring that on all levels, symbolically, mythically, culturally.

The heroine, Cowrie, is as much me as Kerewin is Keri Hulme. I think it is a mistake for people outside the book to see the fictional person as the author because there are real differences there. But yes, always, it's like dreams. Jung says every element, every person who comes into our dreams is a part of us because they've come out of our head, our emotions and our spirit. So in that sense I believe that for every author who creates a character, in some sense those characters are part of them. That's where the spirituality, the magic, the soul interaction happens.

I've used dreams a lot, basing workshops around accessing dreams through writing. The dreams that the students record and write up are a vast source for their subconscious creativity. It provides enough material for a lifetime of writing and can be used in all areas of creativity.

The recurrent dream in *Cowrie* was one I used to have; what I added was the turtle. It was very intuitive. Hanoa, whom I lived with in Hawai'i, told me about Laukiamanuikahiki, Turtle Woman, and it was from these stories that I wove the whole plot. What I didn't know at the beginning was that Turtle Woman was orphaned. It was only in the writing of the book that I discovered it.

I couldn't believe how many parallels there were to the myth of Turtle Woman and Cowrie's own journey of discovery. That was trusting the intuitive.

To write *Cowrie* I had to unlearn everything I've ever learned about writing and everything I ever learned getting a PhD on how other people write. So for me it was a process of honouring spirituality and honouring who I am in writing that book. And I knew the process could fall on its face and that a lot of people would not recognise what I was trying to do. But it has actually touched people on emotional and mythical levels and that's precisely what I was hoping would happen.

And the sensuality — you would have to be pretty shut off not to connect with it, in a very generalised sense. Erotic energy is usually focused on people, but it's out there in the land and ocean and can be tuned into for creative energy. It's a force in the universe and it's how we deal with that force that's interesting.

Caribbean-US writer Audre Lorde said when we refuse the erotic, we deny the YES within ourselves, the force of the creative impulse. Fiction is perhaps the only area in life that we have total freedom to create what we want. How you look at fiction and how you look at the world in spiritual terms connects with this because a lot of people think to have a good novel you must have conflict. It's what I call a patriarchal imperative. So if you write a book in which there is conflict within the main character, conflict between forces of creation and destruction, that is often not recognised as conflict, because it is not externalised in the world. They need some external action conflict, to make it work for them. I find that fascinating because most conflict goes on within us in life. Everything out there is just a reflection of what happens in the mind.

Ethics come into spirituality very strongly when working with writers. Any teacher or guide needs a strong set of ethics because the person coming to them is going to be vulnerable and open out. I think there is a huge responsibility in that.

I don't normally talk publicly about my spirituality. It's something very private to me; it's something that people who know me and work with me and the people who read my books know is there. It's not something I project into the world as a commodity because I don't see it that way.

Heaps of people have been influential in my understanding and development of my spirituality. Going to America was a deep inspiration. I went there on a post-doctoral Fulbright Scholarship. It wasn't a coincidence that I chose the University of California, Berkeley, although all I knew about it at the time was that it was where the freedom of speech movement happened and where a lot of the energy gathered in the sixties.

Berkeley is among the top five percent of US universities and I very much wanted to go there. But what happened was that I realised I was in this huge, multicultural community of healers from very different backgrounds, and from all over the world. It was stimulating and exciting.

There were people who influenced me very much, like Lesley Grey who is a Native American shaman. And I worked with a Kahuna and a

Lomi Lomi healer in Hawai'i. I was also very influenced by the work of African-US healer and storyteller Luisah Teish, who lived three doors away and who now comes to Aotearoa regularly. She taught me the power of oral storytelling, along with storyteller Mona Williams from Guyana, who currently resides in Aotearoa.

Everywhere I went there were people I connected with. I had tremendous support from writers Adrienne Rich, Michelle Cliff, Judy Grahn, Paula Gunn Allen, Joy Harjo and Audre Lorde. These women came from Jewish, Jamaican, New Mexican, Pueblo Sioux, Creek Indian and West Indian ancestry. We talked, danced, sang, read poetry, ate, and shared our cultures together. It was a time of struggle and celebration. I will never forget the influence of these women on my life: they respected and loved me, utterly believed in my work and encouraged me to explore the depths of my creativity as well as supporting others to do so.

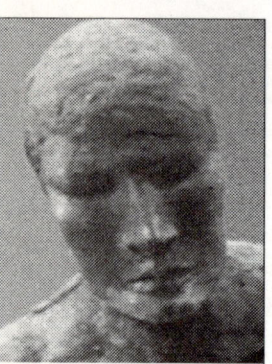

ETHICS COME INTO SPIRITUALITY VERY STRONGLY WHEN WORKING WITH WRITERS.
ANY TEACHER OR GUIDE NEEDS A STRONG SET OF ETHICS.

One moment in particular stands out in my mind. I was staying with Adrienne Rich and Michelle Cliff in their house in Santa Cruz. I'd usually spend a few days with them discussing writing, sharing music and eating wonderful food we'd prepared for each other. This night Michelle had made some superb dolmas — minced lamb, yoghurt and spices wrapped in vine leaves. We went to bed very late, as usual, and I stayed awake till about 2 am, fired with ideas, unable to sleep. I sneaked out to the fridge for more dolmas and Adrienne, also awake, came to do the same. We laughed, realising our hunger was as much for the sharing and ideas as for the food! I showed her some of my wild paintings of fantastic animals and creatures that had entered my dreams. She looked through them intently, with that piercing intelligence and sharpness she has and said: 'Cathie, you are enormously talented. I truly believe you could do anything you really put your heart and soul into.' This, coming from one of the greatest writers in America, and more than that, from a woman whom I deeply admired from the pit of my soul, touched me so deeply I cried.

Now, years later, I have honoured her words, exploring my own creativity in my writing, but also through pottery, photography, painting gourds, weaving shells into kete, etching. The University of Osnabruck published my earth, air, fire and water mandalas in *Survivors: Uberlebende* and they'll be reprinted in a US anthology next year. My first pottery exhibition is upcoming. I'm fired up by pit-firing: working with clay that goes back into the ground to get fired. And I've just been awarded a Creative New Zealand Arts Council grant to write the sequel to *Cowrie*. So I'm spiritually on fire at the moment. The longer I live, the more I see creativity and spirituality as inextricably linked.

On Great Turtle Island (USA) I also worked closely with Penel Thronsen, who was a really big influence in my life. She is a deeply spiritual person who came from Montana and she had an instinctive understanding of indigenous cultures and an understanding of spirituality. She encouraged me to include this in my creativity, in my work with writers and in my own writing and painting. The results can be seen in the Cowrie novels, where I include oral storytelling and my own artwork within the stories.

I think in Aotearoa I would also like to acknowledge people like Juliet Batten, Hinewirangi and Lea Holford, who I think have really put themselves on the line to bring spirituality into focus in a much more conscious sense than I have. I've done it through a lot of different creative roles. Very clearly it's been their main role in life and I think they've influenced many people. I often send writers who come to my courses on to their courses to help free their creativity.

The publishing consultancy has also encouraged the growth of spiritual publications in Aotearoa. Perhaps the best example of this is when two women came to me about five years ago who were working on the first Pacific tarot deck and book. They didn't want to claim indigenous images that weren't theirs, but they wanted to give a Pacific feel to the cards. They're stunning. The Hangman, for instance, is someone bungy-jumping off the Auckland Harbour Bridge and we can see dolphins and sea creatures swimming beneath the water.

We worked on this deck and book for four years, inside and outside paid time. I challenged them on all kinds of levels. I felt there needed to be a stronger gender balance in the deck. We also looked at the naming. I said, 'Why should there be a major arcana and a minor arcana? Let's get rid of the hierarchy in the tarot deck. Let's look at round cards. Let's look at calling them songs. Let's look at reflecting the natural world. You've done that in the imagery, let's do it in the linguistic wording of it.' We worked together brilliantly as a team and it was very exciting. I encouraged Catherine and Dwariko to book a stand at the International Feminist Book Fair and they sold out! They were one of the hits of the book fair. I think it was because people from the Northern Hemisphere had never seen cards like this before, they'd never felt that sort of energy. They were amazed and delighted.

There was no publisher in New Zealand willing to take that one on.

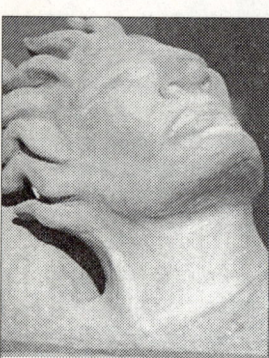

This often happens. The women's project was way ahead of where the publishers were at; they couldn't comprehend a deck of cards that went with a book. I convinced Catherine and Dwariko to do it themselves, with the help of Renée Lang. It's a beautiful production and they've gained a sense of real integrity in putting it out. They do seminars and they're both living off it now. So the Pacific tarot deck *Songs for the Journey Home* was influential for me.

I see working with writers as a mutual experience, where people touch on deep levels, where there's an amazing quality of energy between us. It's magic when I can work like this: it gives me endless energy because I passionately love working as a publishing consultant. I work with a team of writers who mutually support each other. I'm currently working with Renée, Beryl Fletcher and Susan Sayer on a series of writing panels and we are performing at the Wellington and Edinburgh Fringe Festivals. It's work with creativity, spirit and joy. I love working in a team like this. I'm also doing a one-woman performance at the Edinburgh Festival this year at a great venue on Royal Mile, right in the heart of the festival.

I SEE WORKING WITH WRITERS AS A MUTUAL EXPERIENCE, WHERE PEOPLE TOUCH ON DEEP LEVELS, WHERE THERE'S AN AMAZING QUALITY OF ENERGY BETWEEN US.

Other people see the new women's writing collections I put out as being political, but for me they were also spiritual. The first *New Women's Fiction* I worked on in America was like cries for help from women wanting something in their lives, and creativity is where they found it. With over 300 stories submitted, it was hard work. Publishers said it would never sell. But I think if you know that what you're doing is right there's an audience out there. It sold 2000 copies in six weeks and created a record for a New Zealand anthology of new writing.

All the anthologies – *The Exploding Frangipani, Subversive Acts* and *Me and Marilyn Monroe* – have been successful, deeply fulfilling and have bridged a vital gap in the New Zealand psyche. Australian writer and critic Michelle Proctor recently acknowledged this in an international review of books, which is gratifying.

I'm currently co-editing a sequel to *The Exploding Frangipani* with Susan Sayer and Susan Hawthorne called *Car Maintenance, Explosives and Love.* One book feeds and nourishes the next one.

It's been a journey to see how we could get women writers into print. We had to do women's anthologies to get the sort of material that was meaningful because the work that was being chosen for mixed anthologies often wasn't very radical. The well-known writers – Keri Hulme, Shonagh Koea, Frances Cherry, Fiona Kidman, Sue McCauley, and Lauris Edmond – who all helped with the books by contributing work, wrote some of their most powerful pieces in those anthologies. Award-winning films have been made from two of the stories: Frances Cherry's *Waiting For Jim (One Man's Meat)* and Keri Hulme's *Hinekaro.* It's very exciting when one medium inspires another in this way. I admire Christine Parker's ability to transform those stories into provocative and exciting films.

I WISH EVERY AUTHOR COULD HAVE THIS EXPERIENCE, SINCE OUR WORKS ARE SACRED, ARE DEEPLY PART OF OUR-SELVES AND DESERVE THAT KIND OF RESPECT.

The first overtly spiritual book I wrote was commissioned by the University of Osnabruck, Germany. It's an amazing venture because it's in English/Maori and German. The poems are spiritual poems dedicated to women who influenced me deeply, creatively and spiritually, some of whom I talked about earlier. I see the spiritual and the creative intimately connected.

In *Survivors: Uberlebende* are four mandalas, all pre-Pakeha Maori and Hawai'ian symbols that I found on lava rocks and in caves. Hanoa, whom I knew in Hawai'i, took me up to some of the caves there. Some of the symbols were similar to Maori symbols. When I came back to Aotearoa and lived on the land here at Tawharanui in a little shack, I didn't have any hot running water or power so I had to work on the mandalas by candlelight at night. I produced writing paper with the etchings as borders and I sent them back to Germany with letters. It was the Germans who thought of producing the book with these symbols as an integrated part of the text; that indicated cross-cultural input and showed me they were spiritually connected to the work. That poetry collection is the best-selling book produced in the Obema series by the University of Osnabruck Press — so I guess the spiritual can mix happily with the commercial.

In *Cowrie* and *The Journey Home: Te Haerenga Kainga,* the symbols also framed the page. I like the visual to reflect the verbal. I paint and carve and sketch as much as I write. This process of creativity is crucial to me in daily existence.

I like the mixture of genres. Ross Stevens made a really interesting comment when he interviewed me for National Radio's *Anthology* literature programme. He said a lot of New Zealand artists like Colin McCahon have used words in their paintings but he'd never seen symbolic images around words in quite the same way as in *Cowrie.* I didn't see it as something radical, I saw it as a natural extension of what I was doing.

But he's not the only person to have remarked on this. When Keri Hulme launched *Cowrie* at the International Feminist Book Fair she said: 'Throughout Aotearoa and especially in the South you find caves and in the caves you find marvellous drawings and sometimes petroglyphs. Once you have found a cave that has been inscribed, it becomes alive, touched by the human spirit. You all have a special treat in store in reading *Cowrie.* You will find the petroglyphs and drawings play quite a large part in the book. This novel makes an especial mark on New Zealand writing and of course, because she has reached much further afield, on Pacific writing. *Cowrie* is an extraordinary work. There's been nothing like it published in New Zealand before and I deeply suspect not elsewhere. So may the book fare well on its journeys of the world. May it be protected by the turtle spirit that is so openly and magically and poignantly a part of its pages...' (from a video of the *Cowrie* book launch, Melbourne, 1994).

Keri's launch speech was deeply spiritual and sent the book out into the world as a taonga, a sacred gift, 'protected by the turtle spirit'. I wish every author could have this experience, since our works are sacred, are deeply part of ourselves and deserve that kind of respect.

As well as people there have been places that have been influential for me, in Aotearoa and Hawai'i especially. But in the cities of the Northern Hemisphere I found meditation retreats and spiritual activity were happening indoors. Physically and literally, I cannot meditate indoors — I've never been able to do it. So when I'm living in cities like Berlin, London, New York, San Francisco and Amsterdam, I induce images of Aotearoa and Hawai'i, the ocean, the tree ferns, puriri, kereru, tui, the magic dunes of the Hokianga, and Pele's crater at Kilauea, and only then can I fully relax. I've had a lot of writers staying here from overseas and from around Aotearoa. Even if they say they never meditate they sit out in the hot tub under the mamaku and after an hour they'll be into some kind of dream space you couldn't interrupt even if you wanted to.

In Aotearoa we don't generally acknowledge the spiritual in a day-to-day way. I think we are naturally a very spiritual culture but publicly we glorify the material and that's really sad. And yet touch any New Zealander, for example blokes who say, 'I love the family bach,' and find out what it is that they really enjoy. Being out alone fishing: they would never call it spiritual, but it is. There's something unique about the spirituality of Aotearoa — and it's intimately linked with the power of te whenua, the land.

I don't see a split between the spiritual and the political. I don't mean in terms of Labour, National and Alliance, but in terms of our daily lives. I'm talking about why we are sitting here, what's allowed us to be here: that's both spiritual and political. For the political to work it has to have a spiritual underlay and for the spiritual to work it has to have a political underlay. Beyond this is the power of aroha, of love, to heal all of us.

My home is also an expression of my spirituality. And I share this retreat with people who cannot afford to stay in retreat centres. I built this house with three other people. There's something that happens when you actually build your own place and put your energy into it; it has a special quality. For many, this place 'Mohala' (Hawai'ian for Gently Unfolding Creativity) reminds them of their childhood treehuts. It brings out their creativity. When guests come here they write, paint, work with clay, get in touch with their creativity, their spirituality again. It's magic.

I lived in a tin garage here before — without any hot running water or power or toilet. I had a long-drop up the back. When I was living in the tin shack people used to think it was really romantic, especially because they would only come up and see it in summer. It was on the ground, wet, damp, with no drainage; everything would get mouldy and I'd have to clean it every week. But somehow, because I looked as if I was living in poverty, some saw that as being noble. And some people who never saw me living like that have since come to my house and immediately thought I was rich, not realising I have a huge mortgage. So people's concepts of what's correct or not, in a spiritual sense, really interest me. I have since inspired other women to build their own homes, often with

State support. It's crucial that we have our own spaces, shaped by us, to live in.

I think there's a part of the spiritual movement in New Zealand that has an outer face to it and in a sense it is quite commercial, physical and materialistic. You've got to focus your spirituality and I've focused mine in my work; that obviously has a commercial side to it, but it's how you do it and the ethics with which you do it which are vitally important to me.

I OFTEN HAVE TO ENDURE STEREOTYPED IMPRESSIONS OF WHO I AM FROM PEOPLE WHO HAVE NEVER MET ME...

For example, I gave two years' energy to our local community which is a poor, rural, multicultural area. We renovated an old dairy factory at Matakana and now have 63 people on the artists' collective, most of whom were on benefits. That work was a grounding of spirituality in a physical sense for me. It was a particularly hard part of my life, but deeply satisfying.

I have a large, multicultural whanau support system which sustains my daily work. This comprises both blood family and adopted family and includes Caribbean, Maori, Samoan, German-Samoan, Jewish, Black American, Aboriginal, Hawai'ian, Tahitian, Irish, Welsh, Scottish and British people. I feel deeply supported and respected for the work I do and that nurtures me when I read or hear the inevitable criticism that all strong, vocal, empowered women who dare to earth their dreams get from others. I often have to endure stereotyped impressions of who I am from people who have never met me but trot out their homophobic clichés about what they think strong women are like. Of course, this reveals more about where they are coming from than about who I really am. When I'm criticised by others I look at what I have to learn from their comments. I discard the rest.

A lifetime of being a scapegoat as an outspoken feminist resulted in my contracting leukaemia two years ago. Since then I've worked very hard to integrate the spiritual and the political in my life and to act from the power of creativity rather than to react to the disempowering criticism of others – which ultimately only reflects their own self-dissatisfaction. Now I'm healing myself at an amazing rate.

I'm passionately dedicated to the work I do, to my extended whanau and can say I'm deeply happy in life. Every day I enact my politics through my work and my spirituality. It's this integration of action and belief that makes for a feeling of great satisfaction and keeps me always challenging myself and others. Giving birth to Cowrie and putting her out in the world has brought the most amazing and wonderful people into my life. I'm deeply grateful for that. I've also connected with a lifelong Soulmate Lover, who understands me from the inside. She is teaching me about shapes, wordless places and influences my work with clay. We inspire each other with our creativity and share deep aroha. Every day I feel blessed by our closeness. It's a deeply spiritual connection.

I want to encourage other women to explore their creativity and spirit on their own terms. The publishing consultancy is a part of earthing those dreams and empowering others. I urge them to explore their spirit through creativity; it's in us all, it just needs empowering. It lies dormant, like clay: before you breathe into it, shape it into life.

AUDREY SHARP

AUDREY SHARP WAS BORN IN THAMES. HER PARENTS
SHARED A COMMON POLITICAL PHILOSOPHY, ALTHOUGH HER FATHER WAS
A COMMUNIST SOCIALIST AND HER MOTHER'S SOCIALISM
IS BASED IN HER CHRISTIANITY.

Brought up a Christian, she taught Sunday School, motivated more by a desire to be a teacher than religious beliefs. In her teens she felt angry with the patriarchal nature of the church. She became interested in other forms of spirituality, religion and ritual after coming into contact with a witch and seeing her books on witchcraft, spell-making and magic.

Audrey did a masters degree in political science, attended teachers college then taught for some years. She has travelled widely and while in China had an experience which changed her life.

After looking at Buddhism, Hinduism and other religions, she found women's spirituality appealed to her because it fitted in with her sense of individuality. Her spirituality is integrally linked to her socialist politics.

Audrey is developing an organic farm north of Auckland which she plans to be a retreat place in the future. She is bringing up her children to acknowledge Jesus and God in the terms of their father who is Christian, and also to respect the Mother Goddess.

I was born in Thames in 1956. My father was a communist socialist and agnostic/atheist and looked at everything from more of a rationalist point of view. My mother is a Christian and her socialism is based on her Christianity. The two of them with their very different perspectives had a common bond of politics, and it coloured my whole life.

My background is as a practising Christian. My father believed in justice for all people and the need to fight for the underdog, but there was no spirituality in him at all, whereas for my mother, who is still a practising Christian, her spirituality is extremely important to her. But I wouldn't call her a conventional Christian by any means; when I told her I was a witch she commented that it was probably as a result of her being 'basically a bit bent'. My mother was involved in the local church and taught Sunday School; I did as well when I was in the sixth and seventh form, although that was because I wanted to learn to be a teacher rather than for reasons of religious fervour.

I never really fitted in, in Thames. I think it was because my parents stood out as being so different in a small town – they were political and involved in local issues – and I was brought up to be independent and to have opinions of my own from a very early age, which was unusual among children.

I didn't get on very well with my peers. Already in my teens I was becoming angry that the patriarchal nature of the church made so many divisions between men and women – although I didn't recognise it at that stage as being a feminist attitude.

When I was 15 or 16 I had an experience that probably changed my whole life. I was staying with friends and a woman flatting in the house was a practising witch. She had a whole library in her room of books on witchcraft, spell-making and magic. I went searching the bookshops later, looking for these books, but they weren't available in New Zealand at that time. She didn't try to convince me of anything, but the fact she was into something very different intrigued me, and after meeting her I became very interested in other forms of spirituality, religion and ritual. The woman made such an impression on me I named my daughter after her.

At university I did a masters degree in political science. My father had always wanted me to go into politics, but studying it was probably the worst thing I could have done: it put me off going into politics for life.

After attending teachers' college and teaching for a year I travelled on my own for three years through Asia, the Middle East, Europe and North America. On returning to New Zealand I worked with the YMCA in Rotorua for two years on a work-skills programme with unemployed people and I had a lot to do with the Maori community there.

Then I went away again for another year to China, Japan, the Philippines and Hong Kong. For a period of about 10 years, up until that time, I'd had a recurring dream about an old Chinese man who was very wise. It was never clear in the dream if I was one of the people asking his advice or if in fact I was the old man, but I knew it was important that I go to China for my thirtieth birthday and find this old man – I know it sounds a bit weird. Thirty was like a turning point in my life where I left youth and moved into what I called experience.

I went into many holy places and turned 30 in Dunghug and in one of the 500 Magao caves and grottoes I first came into contact with Kwan Yin, who was pictured in the cave. It was significant that when I met her I had started on a whole new area of spirituality.

I later read about Kwan Yin and realised it was her mercy and compassion without expectation which I appreciated. Unlike the Christian God, who demands total belief in one God, Kwan Yin expects nothing and gives everything. It is truly unconditional love. She was the only female deity pictured in the cave; most of the others were male or animal. Buddhism has very patriarchal images.

On the day before I was due to leave China I was in Canton, taking photographs, and a voice called out behind me. It was the man from my dream. He took me to his home and had some words of advice for me: I had to be positive. I had a lot to give in life and I was too bound up with being negative. He said one day I would have a place where I could work from home and there would be many people who would come to where I was. That was why I had to meet him, for he needed to give me this message. This was a major change for me. I take all the problems and injustices of the world to heart; my mother and father taught me to care about my fellow human beings and it had affected my whole attitude to life, making me very negative. But after that things changed quite dramatically.

I was going to teach in China but I had a nagging feeling something wasn't right with my family so I cut my trip short. Within eight weeks of my coming home my father died of cancer. He and I were very close; we had a lot in common and a good understanding of political and historical issues, so his death was a major thing in my life.

My father fought death because although he wanted to die there was nothing for him after life. Seeing him die made me realise there was something missing in my life; despite the intellectual philosophy that I had and the political viewpoints it wasn't enough. It was as if I wasn't quite whole.

After that I attended Lea Holford's course on women's spirituality. I couldn't cope with conventional Christianity and I've looked at Buddhism, Hinduism and other religions, but it had to be something which would fit my individuality. Women's spirituality appealed because you can do it at home, by yourself – you don't have to be in a group. You can create your own spirituality in the life that you live. There's no convention that says it has to be like this or that. Every person can create their own spirituality through the Pagan belief in the Goddess.

I'm very anti the 'new age' ideas because basically a lot of it is so lacking in politics. It's all into doing good and self-truth and self-discovery, but there is no political analysis in there whatsoever. The belief that you can choose your own destiny I think is absolute rubbish. If you are born black in Ethiopia and you come into the world when there's famine, what choice do you have? None! There are people who overcome their environment and sometimes incredible odds, but I think they are exceptions. I'm basically a socialist and think we live in an unjust world with a class system. I feel very strongly that when I see someone who is suffering because of being a woman, or being black, or having a religious viewpoint, it is my responsibility to fight for their right to be what they are.

On the day before I was due to leave China I was in Canton, taking photographs, and a voice called out behind me. It was the man from my dream.

With women's spirituality I can have that analysis and still have my spirituality. I don't see it as 'new age' because there is no abrogating of responsibility. But I think the popular form of women's spirituality alienates a lot of politicised women in the women's movement. This 'touchy-feely' stuff would be anathema to them. Many women are putting their energy into self-growth and self-discovery and that's important; I've done a lot of that myself to deal with things that have happened to me in the past that have been unpleasant – but I believe you should go beyond that.

Ultimately it comes back to the question, Are you part of a community or part of a society? If you are you therefore have to take responsibility for everybody. I think a lot of real feminists are put off because they don't see spirituality as being linked in with a political analysis. It's the same sort of attitude that my father had. He could not accept in himself any core of spirituality, believing the two things were totally alienated. And I disagree. I believe to be a whole person you need to have spirituality, but that doesn't mean you get rid of politics.

A lot of people connect the word 'witch' with negative power, but I like the word because it has a lot of power. A witch is a follower of wicca, a wise woman, and that's what it meant originally. I feel it is important that as a woman I am going back to ancestral traditions that my family probably practised generations ago. I reclaim the word 'witch' and I like the reaction it gets when I use it, because I can immediately explain what it means and increase other people's understanding of it.

WHEN I CAME OUT AS A WITCH THERE WAS AN ARTICLE ABOUT ME, THERE WAS AN INCREDIBLE AMOUNT OF FUSS IN THE SMALL COMMUNITY IN WHICH I LIVE.

When I came out as a witch and there was an article about me in the *New Zealand Herald*, there was an incredible amount of fuss in the small community in which I live. My mother, who is involved with the Church, got a hard time; no one talked to me about it but they did to her, which was unfair.

Ritual is very important for me; it allows me to work through a lot of things going on in my head and my heart in a way that is very safe. I use the elements of fire, earth, air and water in a ritualistic way. It may be very simple; for example, you can write what's bugging you on a piece of paper, put it in a fire and burn it. If you say some words with it and acknowledge what you are doing, it will go.

I do a lot of ritual at home because many in my ritual group, Hags, which is an Auckland-based group, have moved away. We don't get together very often but I still feel a very strong connection with those women. We occasionally meet for a ritual but I don't feel the need now to be in a group, though when I started I did. I feel I've integrated my spirituality so much into my life now that if I have a need, if there's something I need to work through, I can do my own ritual. I either go up to the top of the farm where there's lots of space, which I need because I am an air person, or I'll do something in the barn where I work with fire, my other element.

Often I create a circle, setting out the elements, and I call to the appropriate goddess, spirit power or energy source that I'm wanting to invoke.

I make some sort of declaration of purpose and say what I'm asking for. I might get up and dance or write something on a piece of paper, then set it alight, or do something with water, scattering it around. I chant and that's very important because it creates an energy cone: I do a lot of chanting down by the stream, which is a very special place. The trees have spirits.

I dowsed this land before I bought it, to search for water and find out whether it was a good place to be. The land had been terribly hurt – raped, as women are raped. The goats that lived on the farm before I bought it had stripped it not only of weeds but also of much of the bush. With their departure the regrowth has been tremendous and I have planted over a thousand trees in four years. The land smiles at what I am doing, the trees tell me that they are pleased and all that I plant is thriving.

I look towards sustainability – sustainability of the land and of myself, integrating my spirituality within all I do and what I am, using creative expression through sound and dance. It is wonderful chanting down by the stream or up on top of the hill by the mother crystal.

I carry out most of the formal rituals up on the top ridge. I have a sun sign and I find being up on the ridge with all the air very cleansing because it allows my mind to be free. Another element that is important to me is fire because my moon is a fire sign and the moon is very powerful. In the barn I light candles, using different-coloured candles for different occasions. If I'm doing a ritual in the winter-time I use black candles for invoking Hecate or Kali, the goddess who is from under the earth, who will be happy to talk with the spirits of the dead and who guards the underworld. In the springtime I'd probably use green candles, because green is associated with birth and rebirth. If I was wanting to do something to evoke Venus energy, the love energy, I'd use red.

When I taught women's spirituality classes in 1992, every week we had a different theme and I used different candles and ribbons for each. I would set up an altar with the colour of the ribbon around the altar and the colour of the candles and symbols I placed there would be chosen according to what I was doing. I have a Kwan Yin goddess I use a lot: she is the goddess of mercy and compassion and is very important to me because I feel a strong sense of connection to China. But also of all the goddesses she is totally compassionate.

I like goddesses, spirits, energy forces that don't demand too much. The Goddess appeals to my whole sense of wanting freedom to do my own thing. She doesn't expect anything of me – I can call on her power and she'll be there for me. I also use something similar to the I Ching, the Kwan Yin Book of Changes written by an American woman called Diane Stein, using it rather as people use the tarot. It's a very feminist book with positive messages; there's no negativity in it, which appeals to me because I think what counts is how you view things. You could look at death and say it's negative, but if we didn't have death we wouldn't have birth — death and rebirth are part of a cycle. I like Kwan Yin energy because it sees there is positive in all things and thus relates to the message that the old man gave me.

I LOOK TOWARDS
SUSTAINABILITY —
SUSTAINABILITY OF
THE LAND AND
OF MYSELF,
INTEGRATING MY
SPIRITUALITY WITHIN
ALL I DO...

That positiveness is something I need to keep in the forefront of my mind because I can easily get depressed knowing that I live in a world that is very polluted; I know that once my whole farm was kauri and I can see where they dragged all the kauri trees down the back. Also, I know that terrible things happen like the abuse of children who don't have an advocate and can't fight for themselves.

By having a 30-year plan for the farm I feel very strongly that in working towards that goal I can do my little bit to try to make the world a better place. We are creating an organic farm and eventually this whole place will be set up with workshops and places for people to come and retreat, giving them a chance to look at where they are and try to integrate and balance their life and the elements within them. For me, balance is the key.

I am involved in the local community, supporting and developing local projects as well as teaching business skills, accounting, book-keeping and political economy. On one level this doesn't fit with my philosophy because I feel business is exploitative and has been responsible for a lot of the destruction that has taken place on the planet. But at the same time I live in an area where there are a lot of unemployed people who want to do something for themselves and can't afford to pay a high-powered consultant. We work out a deal, often bartering.

Communicating my sense of spirituality to my daughter is a bit tricky, as her father is a Christian and it causes some debate in our life. She has been to rituals with me and we talk about it around the house, but she's a bit young yet so I'm waiting for the time she asks me about it. It's going to be very obvious that her father's viewpoint and mine are totally different. My daughter acknowledges Jesus and God in her father's terms, but respects the Mother and Goddess. She also connects with unicorns and I encourage that openness and imagination in her.

My son has brought male energy onto the farm in another way. His coming has also brought a balance in my own mothering role. The energies of my two children are very different and they are each teaching me about what it is to be a mother.

I know and understand the Maiden and Crone. The Mother is my own challenge and I hope with the help of my children and the Great Mother of us all I will learn to integrate her within myself.

JULIET BATTEN

JULIET BATTEN WAS BORN IN INGLEWOOD, GREW UP IN TARANAKI
AND MOVED TO AUCKLAND WHEN SHE WAS 14 YEARS OLD.
HER PARENTS SENT HER TO SUNDAY SCHOOL AT THE ANGLICAN CHURCH,
WHERE SHE WAS CONFIRMED.
IN LATER YEARS AT HIGH SCHOOL SHE STOPPED GOING TO CHURCH
AND AT UNIVERSITY TURNED HER BACK ENTIRELY ON RELIGION.
BUT AFTER MARRYING AT 20 HER LOVE OF ART
TOOK HER TO EUROPE WHERE SHE VISITED THE GREAT CATHEDRALS
AND MONASTERIES AND STOOD IN AWE BEFORE THE PAINTINGS AND FRESCOES
OF MANY OF THE MASTERS OF THE CHRISTIAN TRADITION.
WHILE LIVING IN CORNWALL AND OTHER PARTS OF BRITAIN
SHE VISITED STONEHENGE AND EVERY STONE CIRCLE
AND ANCIENT SITE SHE COULD LOCATE,
NOT KNOWING THEN THAT THEY WERE GODDESS SITES.

Back in New Zealand, she completed an MA and then a PhD on Thomas Hardy and his debt to the visual arts. After living for two years in Paris she returned to Aotearoa where she began to develop her art work. At the same time her involvement in the environmental movement resulted in her teaching environmental studies at Auckland University for a number of years. She then moved into women's studies, teaching a wide range of creative workshops and developing collaborative art projects for women, the largest of which was the ritualistic 100 Women Project at Te Henga Beach. This was part of her ongoing work with site installation on the land, involving processes of tide, wind, erosion and seasonal change.

Juliet has held many solo exhibitions as well as being part of group shows. In 1990 she was an invited artist in the Mana Tiriti exhibition for which she led a large ritual. She has also made videos and done performance art.

Her publications include *Songs of the Green Snake, Crone-ologies: Women Emerging Through Menopause, Power From Within: A Feminist Guide to Ritual* and *Celebrating the Southern Seasons: Rituals for Aotearoa.*

Her travels have also taken her to India, the United States and Ireland. Since 1983 she has practised meditation. She now works as a psychotherapist, artist and writer in Auckland. She has a son and a granddaughter.

Making rituals was something that happened spontaneously. It came out of my work as an artist.

When I think about it I've made rituals since I was a little girl. I used to make a fairy ring on the grass, leave my tooth under it and my aunt would put a sixpence there in the morning. I was always working with rituals and magic quite naturally when I was a child growing up in Taranaki.

I had that sense of relationship with the land when I came to live at Te Henga on Auckland's west coast. In my work as an artist I worked naturally with the elements and as I began to use the sand and the sea and different elements I found myself letting these works become quite ritualistic, going through rituals before I made them and then making rituals of letting them go back to the elements.

Ever since my childhood I felt a profound connection with the natural world: the bush, the iron-sand beaches and the mountain Taranaki that watched over my growing up. Later, when Te Henga became my second spiritual home, to shape the sand in collaboration with the incoming tide seemed as natural as breathing, a continuity with a way of connecting that I had always known.

In the late seventies, through my art work I became involved with ritual and the rituals became more and more conscious. Then I began to read about ritual in other cultures and understand, also through my own experience, that ritual moves through a process and a sequence of events that allow a ritual to happen, and a deep transformation to occur.

The other thing that happened through which ritual was born for me was my collective art work with women. When we needed to take down a work that had been made together there was a sense of anxiety in a group. There had to be a letting-go of this wonderful art work that they had made and I knew it called for a ritual. So ritual was spontaneously born out of the need at the time.

This first happened with the Lifescape Project at the Auckland Society of Arts in 1982. I suggested to everyone we just pause and contemplate what was happening. We were in a process of transition and I later learned rituals are called for whenever we go through transitions. So I told the women to cut with scissors little pieces from the art environment that represented the essence of the experience. We had a long piece of paper in which each had made a circle and we placed our pieces in that circle, thus making our own new form out of the old. That was the essence of what we were going to carry away with us. We sat and talked about it and what it had been. We photographed our magic circles and then everyone took down the piece with the greatest of ease; all the anxiety had gone. That taught me about the power of ritual to ease the passage of a transition.

WHEN I THINK ABOUT IT I'VE MADE RITUALS SINCE I WAS A LITTLE GIRL. I USED TO MAKE A FAIRY RING ON THE GRASS, LEAVE MY TOOTH UNDER IT...

In 1982 I spent two months in California on an Arts Council grant to study the women's art movement, particularly collaborative art. I was surprised to find there were few truly collaborative projects happening there and that they were interested in my work with collaboration and with nature, especially the way I worked on the beach. I was invited to give slide shows and to do a beach workshop — sand work — with the Women's Building Collective in San Francisco.

I became aware of the women's spirituality movement there, but I did not join in any rituals, nor did I know a lot about what was happening, even though it was very much 'around'. I brought back Sharlene Spretnak's *Politics of Spirituality* and Diane Marichild's *Motherwit* and many other similar books from San Francisco.

Reading these books, and others by Z Budapest and Starhawk, has been influential. Allie Eagle has been an influence too in that she showed me how sand can be a legitimate art form. She came to live in my bach at

Te Henga in the late seventies and was working with the bush and sand in ways that I found inspirational.

I was in a ritual group in 1984 where four of us committed ourselves to celebrating the eight seasonal rituals of the year. We went through the whole year, taking turns at creating the ritual. That was part of the process of becoming more conscious, then I began to teach ritual in 1984, the same year that Lea Holford came to Auckland and also started to teach it. It was so much in the air.

I used ritual in the Menstrual Maze in 1983, The Hundred Women Project in 1985 and The Threshold Project in 1987. So for me the creative process and the making of rituals have always gone together. The ritual-making has been a creative process in itself, arising as a response to a need on a particular occasion, whether it was out on a west coast beach with 100 women or in an art gallery where a show is about to begin — or even in how I present my art work to the public.

THERE'S BEEN AN INTERWEAVING BETWEEN RITUAL, ART AND POLITICS AND THAT'S BEEN IMPORTANT.

In 1989 I had an exhibition called Sacred Spaces and I provided a ritual opening for everybody to participate in who came to the exhibition. They were invited to take stones or shells that I had gathered at Totaranui, where I had done the original artworks. The pieces were ritualistically done on a beach, after which I photographed them, then made colour copies which I pasted onto paper and painted around.

People were asked to place stones, shells or coloured calico on pieces of white muslin underneath any painting they particularly responded to. So by the end of two weeks there were beautiful little installations that had been created by the passing visitors. You could tell which paintings gave rise to the greatest response and what kind of response the paintings evoked because the pieces under each painting were very different.

So for me the rituals have been a part of how to approach art work and how to relate to it in a way that's not like that dead walking around the art gallery as if you are looking at a television screen.

Again, when I did paintings for the exhibition Mana Tiriti, with the theme of the Treaty of Waitangi, I wanted to offer ritual as part of the art-making. The works were created ritualistically as installations on the land. For example, I journeyed to Waitangi and made a piece at the foot of the flagstaff the day after the 1990 Waitangi Day celebrations. It was like a memorial wreath laid there. I went to the beaches and inscribed the words 'Promises' and watched the sea take the words away; then they became part of the art works.

When the works were exhibited up here as part of Mana Tiriti in Auckland, I wanted a big ritual to enable Pakeha to address their own relationship with the land and the people who had gone before. As part of that ritual people brought trees which they offered and which were taken out to Ngati Te Ata people at Maioro, south of Auckland.

There's been an interweaving between ritual, art and politics and that's been important. A lot of the ritual work around Mana Tiriti was about how I can use ritual to help people to release what they need to release so they can move through their blocks and they can act politically. It was to enable Pakeha to overcome their paralysis and take political action – and they did: there was a lot of letter writing and money being sent, for example.

I began teaching ritual classes in 1984 and since then I've taken at least one or two ritual classes every year. I must have taught hundreds and hundreds of women. I've also developed a course called 'Seven Weeks With the Goddess' that uses rituals based around the different Greek goddesses.

This class is a chance to explore each goddess archetype and find out what she represents for us; for example, Hestia is the inward focus. To have a ritual around that focus we need to connect with that energy, so each class evening has a very different energy. I make a centrepiece in the room which speaks of the particular goddess we are studying; for example, when we are studying Aphrodite the room is full of roses, to conjure up the sensuousness of love.

And so we have the ritual and imbibe the energy of that goddess and then our task for the week is to learn what that goddess has to teach us. The next week everyone reports back how they got on, because I am very interested in how we ground this energy and integrate it into our lives.

Usually the women find there are certain of the goddess energies they are very at home with and others they are not. The warriors who, with Athena as their goddess, fight out in the world, may not know about Hestia, the goddess who turns quietly within and knows solitude. Or, they may not know about Demeter, who is about nurturing energy – the self-mothering energy. And so at the end we do an integration ritual, bringing together the missing energies, bringing the weaker ones into the stronger, always moving towards wholeness. The question 'How can we find wholeness?' is a theme which runs through most of our ritual-making.

Over the past few years I've been asked to go round the country taking ritual workshops called 'Creativity and Ritual'. On the first day of the workshop we use the creative process, working together collaboratively as well as on our own. When the creative process has awoken I take people into ritual on the second day, because for me those two – ritual and creativity – are closely connected.

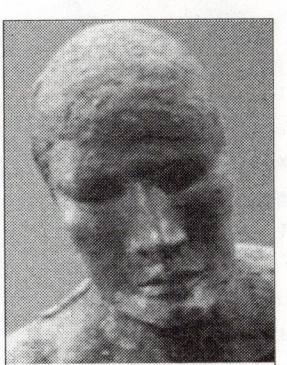

Once the creative process is awakened people will work very naturally with ritual. They discover to their amazement they can make rituals, sacred spaces and wonderful altars. They find they have it in them; it's finding the place to reach to bring it out from that is the important thing.

So in those workshops I am not saying how to do it, or what to do, but I am trying to help people to find that in themselves. It's been wonderful going around the country teaching women for whom this is quite new; they find with great delight that they can do it and afterwards they write to tell me they've carried on making rituals.

IN SOME WAYS WOMEN'S SPIRITUALITY HAS A SIMILAR PHILOSOPHY TO THAT HELD BY MAORI, SUCH AS THE WAY IT FOLLOWS THE CYCLE OF THE SEASONS...

A lot of these women are in rural communities. They say, 'Before when a cow died the children were sad and we didn't know what to do. Now we know we can have a ritual of grieving.' For example, people decide they want to remember the cow so they ask all the children to bring a symbol or draw a picture of what the cow meant to them and how it made them feel. They might bury those symbols in the ground or they might light a candle and blow it out to say goodbye to the cow. They will mark the passing. They may even have a burial of course of the actual animal, and have a ritual afterwards. Rural women and men connect very naturally with life and seasonal processes and I find in many ways they take to ritual very naturally.

The essence of my teaching is for people to discover that they can create their own rituals. All they need to know are certain useful processes.

I wrote an article once for *Womanscript* which I called 'Rituals and the Penguin Cookbook'.

My approach was not about having the kind of cookbook where you follow the recipe and have to get it right; the *Penguin Cookbook* that I learned to cook from as a young woman taught you the method to use and then it said you can have all these variations on the method. The moment I knew the method for making a gravy or a sauce I invented my own sauces and have done so ever since; but first I needed to know the method.

And so with my ritual teaching: it's about teaching the method and giving the experience. It's like once you've had a taste of good food you know what good food tastes like; so after you've had a taste of good ritual you know what you are aiming for, and the rest just happens.

There have been changes over the years. Women now come to the basic ritual class that I began teaching all those years ago in a state of readiness that I would then have considered made them suitable for an advanced workshop. The morphic field is resonating and ritual gets easier and more available the more it's taught.

The rituals have become more inclusive of men and children. For years we concentrated on doing it just for women because we needed to build our spiritual power and reclaim it. Now it's so strong it doesn't matter who we do the rituals with, because we are holding our power.

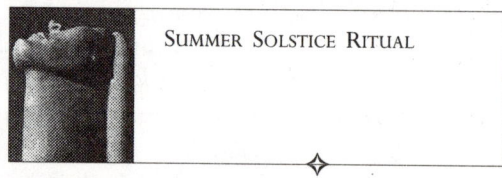

SUMMER SOLSTICE RITUAL

One summer solstice I did a ritual for my group Cone, their partners and children, and wrote a legend about the return of the Sun King from the north. One of the men dressed as the Sun King in a yellow cloak and crown and came up from the bottom of the garden looking resplendent with a clothes-basket full of gifts.

We went out on the balcony and rang bells and clanged brass as a signal for the Sun King to appear. He arrived and gave us our gifts and the message: 'Folks, it doesn't snow here. This is the summer solstice and I bring the sun's energy, the energy of the season and it's a warm, radiant, outgoing energy. It's very compatible with gift giving.' The children loved it. We all circle-danced around the orange tree which was in fruit and hung sun symbols from it. That was a wonderful family ritual.

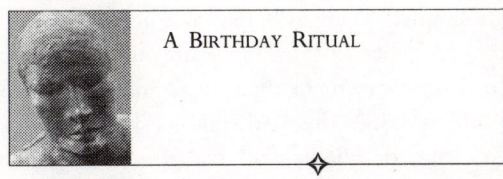

A BIRTHDAY RITUAL

For my fiftieth birthday I had a ritual that was for men and women. The age range was just over a 50-year span, from 21 to 72, and it was a ritual in which I very much wanted to include men because it was about ageing. I wanted men to be there to identify the negative messages about women getting older, with women doing the same, and then all together we would burn these messages.

We wrote the messages on pieces of paper; people brought newspaper cuttings and magazine images as well, and everyone came forward and burned them in three big cauldrons while I stood on my head and watched. The men played the drums, so there was a lot of support between the men and the women, with the women leading the ritual and men doing some of the drumming.

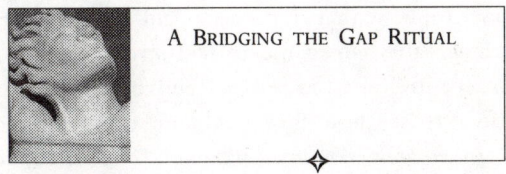

A BRIDGING THE GAP RITUAL

In 1988 I did a ritual called 'Bridging the Gap' about the meeting of male and female energies and what happens when the two meet. We each brought a symbol for female energy and a symbol for male energy and put them in circles of their own. It was fascinating because there was a definite coherence – although there were the odd ones that didn't fit at all, which also felt right. We had a visualisation and drew an image of the meeting-point. There were lots of images of bridges and of sparks flying.

That ritual was held early on when men were just beginning and since then I've held off a little because now men have been starting to get their own work together. They are going through a lot of processes with men's workshops, but I think they have a journey to make before they can come in and meet the women in ritual work, leading together. I think something quite exciting is going to happen.

I have become trained as a counsellor and psychotherapist — a psychosynthesis therapist. This has helped me become more aware of what is happening to my clients as they move through the process of therapy which enables them to transform their lives and themselves. I work as a psychotherapist and combine this with my creative work. Often I use ritual work with clients, or clients will take on ritual when they've been through a major life transition.

Psychosynthesis is a way of working with change that involves the whole person and it works on all levels — body, feelings, mind and soul. It's unlike other psychologies in that it addresses the spiritual dimension; it's been called psychology with a soul.

When I discovered it I knew immediately this was for me, because I had done psychological processes before that didn't bring in the spiritual dimension. I had a spiritual life that didn't address psychological issues sufficiently and suddenly they came together and were synthesised. It was very powerful.

I think psychosynthesis has deepened my understanding of the transformative processes. It's enabled me to be more confident about going deeper with my rituals, and higher. It's given me a sense of confidence in my own power which has been very important, because doing ritual work is about being very visible with my power. And the work I have done in psychosynthesis has really helped me to feel strong in that.

My new work centres on the seasons and brings together Maori and European traditions to see how they might meet here in Aotearoa today. After my book *Power From Within: A Feminist Guide to Ritual Making* was published in 1988, people wrote to me asking for more information about the seasons. I intended to produce a slim volume on the winter solstice, but the project grew and after three years it resulted in a new book, *Celebrating the Southern Seasons: Rituals for Aotearoa*, which was published in 1995.

Ritual offers the container for safe meeting, whether it is between people from different spiritual traditions, of different gender and age or of different race. I continue to be excited and amazed at what can take place when the spiritual container is strong.

RUTH GARDNER

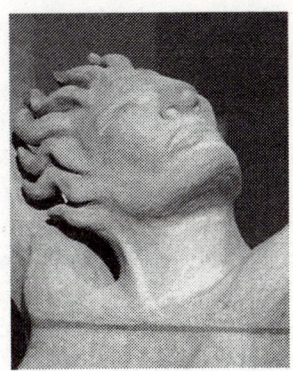

RUTH GARDNER WAS BORN IN AUCKLAND, BUT SHORTLY AFTERWARDS
HER FAMILY MOVED BACK TO CHRISTCHURCH, WHERE SHE LIVED
UNTIL SHE WAS 10 YEARS OLD. SHE AND HER MOTHER THEN WENT BACK
TO AUCKLAND. DURING HER EARLY TEENS SHE LIVED IN THE
THEOSOPHICAL COMMUNITY AT MOUNT ST JOHN AND ATTENDED
EPSOM GIRLS GRAMMAR SCHOOL.
PREGNANT AT 16, RUTH MARRIED AND BROUGHT UP TWO DAUGHTERS
WHILE WORKING AS AN OFFICE MANAGER.
IN 1986 SHE AND HER HUSBAND RETURNED TO CHRISTCHURCH
AND THEY NOW LIVE IN A 130-YEAR-OLD COTTAGE IN THE INNER CITY
WITH THEIR TWO CATS.
RUTH CURRENTLY MANAGES THE CANTERBURY VOLUNTEER CENTRE.

When I think about spirituality the word that comes to mind is 'connections'. My spirituality connects me to life itself, to the past, the future, to every other form of life, to nature and her seasons and cycles, to my family and friends and to a wider universe.

My spirituality is female, it's to do with my being a woman and the special connection I have with the life force because I am a woman. It means honouring models of female divinity and being aware that I am part of that divinity. It's also about the need to bring feminine and masculine into balance. I believe this is vital if we are to have peace and indeed the survival of life.

The ways which I express my spirituality have changed and evolved during my life. I was bought up as a member of the Liberal Catholic (Protestant) Church, and I also had contact with the Theosophical Society. My mother was a lifelong member of the society and we lived in a Theosophical community from the time I was 13. As a child and a teenager I enjoyed going – only irregularly – to church and experienced a sense of mystery, almost trance, during the services. Some of this was due to the fact that my father had died when I was five, and when there was mention of a father in heaven who loved me and was all-knowing, I took it very personally. In my early twenties, after I had married and had two daughters, I realised one day during a service that the sense of mystery had gone and the service meant nothing, so I stopped going.

For the next 10 years or so I was not conscious of my spirituality at all. Looking back I realise that in fact it was expressed in my mothering, my love of gardening and my caring for my pets, cats and hens especially. But at that time I was focused on domesticity and paid work and had no spiritual awareness.

In the mid-seventies I joined the Values Party and I see that as being the beginning of an awareness of spirituality for me as an adult. All the philosophy seemed right; I welcomed it intuitively as well as intellectually, and it gave me the sense of connection which has now become so important to me. Looking at society in a holistic way, realising that the way something is done is as important as achieving the goal – all this resonated within me at a very deep level, feeding an inner hunger of which I'd been unaware. So I channelled my energies, including my spiritual energy, into trying to save the world, or at least into thinking globally and acting locally. For me, political action is an essential part of spirituality, and I still get a sense of inner fulfilment from it, even these days when I'm just doing a few hours a week of telephone canvassing for the Green Party/Alliance.

Being involved with Values also gave my feminism a boost, and I started to attend some women's studies workshops and courses. In 1983 I finally became involved in a consciousness-raising group, much later than many others, but this was the first time that the opportunity and the inclination had come together for me. In the early 80s I started to read about women's spirituality, starting with Merlin Stone's *The Paradise Papers*, which I picked up at a women's studies seminar, and then went on to the writings of Z Budapest and Starhawk.

In 1984 Lea Holford's women's spirituality course was advertised by Continuing Education in Auckland and I thought perhaps I'd go. However

I did not enrol until a few days before it started and was astounded to be told it was booked out. It had never occurred to me that so many other people might also be interested in the subject. I enrolled very early for Lea's 1985 course.

Around the same time I saw Juliet Batten's WEA course in feminist ritual advertised, enrolled for that as well and took part in her '100 Women' event in May 1985. This, along with the rituals in Lea's course, filled a need and fed my soul. I'll never forget the final initiation in Lea's course, and still carry in my wallet the card which was a part of the initiation. I experienced something very special – again that sense of connection – with millions of women who have known the mysteries through the ages. When another woman from the class told me afterwards it had had little effect on her I could hardly believe it. As a result of Lea's class we formed a group called Tapestry and from Juliet's class another group called Cone. For the next 18 months I was a member of both groups, each of which met about once every three weeks. I felt rather greedy belonging to two, but was aware I would be leaving Auckland at the end of 1986 and I wanted all the ritual I could get.

I FELT RATHER GREEDY BELONGING TO TWO GROUPS, BUT WAS AWARE I WOULD BE LEAVING AUCKLAND AND WANTED ALL THE RITUAL I COULD GET.

I was learning to plan and facilitate rituals in both these groups. At the end of 1985 I was part of a group that organised a summer solstice ritual for 90 women and in 1986 a group of six of us organised a women's spirituality weekend for 40 people. Both were amazing experiences. Through all this time I became more and more aware of my own personal power, which was nurtured and shared by other women. The culmination for me was the farewell ritual I gave for Tapestry just before I left Auckland, which was also the end – the last stitch – of Tapestry itself.

At that stage there were only five of us left in the group and the closeness and deepness was wonderful. Cone also taught me a great deal, but it was a different group entirely. Both Juliet and Lea have been empowering teachers; Lea is particularly special, because she has the whole psychological focus. As well as facilitating ritual she is able to analyse what happens, and her approach helped me to go further.

So I came south and missed my ritual groups. I made a couple of attempts to start something here, but nothing really eventuated until with some other friends I attended a 'Women's Ministries and Spirituality' conference in 1988. After this some friends were eager to join me and with a few new women we started a group which has continued to the present, although it has gone through a number of transitions. My experience of ritual was a useful catalyst, but the others very soon caught on. Some of us have also offered rituals which are open to larger groups of women. These days we are Lunatrix, a small, closed group of four that tends to amalgamate with another group of a dozen or so for main festivals. Although our number is small we have resisted admitting anyone else because the link between us is so strong and deep.

I had always felt extremely privileged to have had the grounding in ritual and feminist spirituality which I got from Lea and Juliet and wished there could be something comparable in Christchurch. Part of my expression of spirituality is a strong desire to give other women the opportunity to experience and learn about ritual and the Goddess. I am very aware that I was lucky and that it can be very hard for women to make contact with other women who are also interested.

So I've been motivated to offer larger, open rituals to facilitate new groups, to be available to the media when they want a 'witch', and in 1992 offer a course in women's spirituality. That year a friend and I tutored two six-week courses, and in 1994 I did another one at the local Women's Centre.

That has now been taken over by another member of Lunatrix and I am delighted that there are regular, low-cost courses available and that there is an accessible place where women can get a taste of what women's spirituality can be.

For the past three years I've been working in the non-profit area – currently I manage the Canterbury Volunteer Centre – and have done very little outreach spiritual work, except for one 'croning' ritual for a woman who found me through our Green Dollar Exchange.

Until about three years ago I was working in the commercial area as an administration manager for a chain of retail stores but I became more and more uncomfortable with that. I wanted very much to move into the non-profit area. When I was looking at what I might do I looked quite seriously at offering ritual for fees and started to do so in a very small way, but since I've had paid work in the non-profit area I've not felt the same need. Sometime in the future I might do it because it is definitely something I want to do, but in the meantime, since where I work is helping people and I am not seeking to make a profit, it satisfies me.

Over the last few years I have had four people very close to me die in my immediate family and each time the funeral has been better because I've been able to take more control. The last one was my mother's funeral, last October. It was a good funeral, satisfying and very powerful, as was my brother's funeral, the year before. At these times of immense emotional turmoil, particularly my brother's death, I've been very affirmed by finding I have a great deal of inner strength and that I can rise to the occasion, even though I am full of grief and people around me are in crisis and needy.

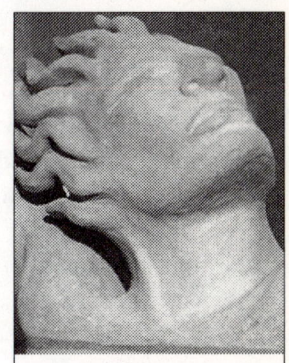

Particularly at my brother's death, I felt that I drew on a spiritual power which is inside me. I see the Goddess but I also see myself embodying the Goddess and I draw great strength from that inner core, which is of course connected to other things outside me.

PART OF MY EXPRESSION OF SPIRITUALITY IS A STRONG DESIRE TO GIVE OTHER WOMEN THE OPPORTUNITY TO EXPERIENCE AND LEARN ABOUT RITUAL AND THE GODDESS.

My mother's funeral last year was truly wonderful and that was because I wrote every word of it myself and expressed the things I wanted to say, and because it was about her and she had given me permission to do it, even though it certainly wasn't a conventional funeral. Most of the people there were my friends rather than hers. The feedback I got was great. A man who was the partner of one of my friends and hadn't experienced anything like that before said he would like his funeral to be exactly the same. His partner said to him 'even the bits about the Goddess?' He said, 'Yes, even that!'

My mother was influential in my spirituality to some extent, even though we didn't really share it. But certainly my whole upbringing left me open to other forms of religion and with a very open mind and I think that has helped.

Other people who have been influential in my life are the women with whom I've shared ritual and the ones who are still sharing that. They are very special to me. I always think of Barbara Stanley and Jill McLaren from Auckland as my two crones. They taught me a great deal in the time I was in a group with them. I have missed having that older woman figure with the kind of wisdom that they have and since I've been down here I've never quite been able to replace their role in my life. The other person who has been influential has been the actual Goddess whom I know in so many different guises both in the past and the present.

I think that spirituality is expressed in creativity and I don't do a lot of art work. When I do I'm very satisfied with it and again I think it's expressing something that needs to come out; that's not an intellectual, but an intuitive thing. Some of that is to do with the garden; walking in nature, all those things when you can feel those connections. That's when my spirituality is expressed: also in physical exercise and dance. Over the years I've quite often taken part in Dances of Universal Peace. I also write some verse.

WALKING IN NATURE, ALL THOSE THINGS WHEN YOU CAN FEEL THOSE CONNECTIONS. THAT'S WHEN MY SPIRITUALITY IS EXPRESSED: ALSO IN PHYSICAL EXERCISE AND DANCE.

My spirituality is linked to my own self-development, so that places that have a meaning for me have a spiritual meaning. When I moved to the South Island there was a connection again with my family, none of whom are here now; but just being in the place where they had been gave me a real sense of spiritual belonging. There is also a connection with nature, all the places where you can feel the elements: being outside.

I remember particularly an open area above the coast on Waiheke Island, where we had a ritual that was the culmination of a Tapestry weekend and which was the first time I felt moved to remove some of my clothes and enjoy the feel of air on my body. There was a Beltane ritual in a park on the Port Hills above Christchurch, where we leapt over a fiery cauldron. But there are also places where I've just been and been able to just be — and perhaps again to be able to go away to some place else inside myself.

Being near water is very important. In Auckland I lived where I could see the sea — just — and in Christchurch I live beside the river. I need that connection. I think I would not now be happy to live anywhere I couldn't see, and be beside, water. I keep coming back to it, but it is still the 'connection'. I have a number of friends and family who are a long way away and the water links me with them. That's something that I often think of: that the water flows everywhere throughout the world, so that the water links us. If I am missing people, just to be by the water and say, 'This water will flow to them as well,' helps me.

I hope that the future will see me having more connection and sharing my spirituality with more people. I'm very keen that other people have the opportunity to experience ritual and also to share with other people because there is a great strength when we get together and it may not only be in ritual. There's often a sense, particularly in a group of women, that there's an extra energy. Because we are together there is something added. That need not specifically be a spiritual focus, but it is an energy that I see as being spiritual. And it doesn't have to be only women; I still get it with a lot of the kind of men I knew in Values and with my own partner. There's something more than the sum of the parts. And I want to experience that more.

I'd like to share my spirituality with more people in more ways and I'd like to have more chances to be creative and have more balance in my life. The idea of my spirituality being shared as widely as it possibly can links back to the political part and the need for balance in the world. I suppose I feel that if I can be loving and live in a good way, then that will spread. So some of the sharing is trying to spread a positive influence that eventually may bring about world peace, as trite as that may sound.

I've talked a little about exploring and choosing and having options and for me that is what is needed to balance the patriarchal side, in which people are directed. I would like everybody to know what the options are and to make an informed and empowering choice, to exercise their own 'power from within' rather than having power imposed over them.

RAEWYNNE

RAEWYNNE WAS BORN IN HUNTERVILLE, THE YOUNGEST OF FIVE CHILDREN
AND THE ONLY GIRL. SHE LATER MOVED TO OTAKI, THEN WELLINGTON,
DUNEDIN AND CHRISTCHURCH, AND BACK TO WELLINGTON
IN HER EARLY TWENTIES.
SHE HAD NO FORMAL CHRISTIAN UPBRINGING.
WHEN SHE WAS SIX HER FATHER LEFT AND HER MOTHER WENT OUT TO WORK.
THE EXPERIENCE OF LIVING IN A RELATIVELY POOR FAMILY
TAUGHT HER BASIC SURVIVAL SKILLS EARLY ON AND TO LISTEN TO
HER OWN INTUITION. HER MOTHER MARRIED AND SHE BECAME
PART OF A MERGED FAMILY OF 10, OF WHICH SHE WAS THE YOUNGEST
UNTIL TWO CHILDREN WERE ADOPTED.
SHE HAD HER FIRST CHILD, A SON, AT 19 AND NOW HAS FOUR CHILDREN,
THREE GIRLS AND A BOY.
RAEWYNNE HAS PROFESSIONAL EXPERIENCE IN THE TELEVISION INDUSTRY
AND THESE DAYS SHE LIVES IN WELLINGTON.

I've been aware since I was very young that I was different; I always knew
that the veils between the worlds made reality not quite what it seemed
to be in terms of physical reality. I used to see little creatures on the beach
and in the garden and I could hear voices when nobody else could hear
them – all the classic psychic child things.

My spirit guides and teachers came to me when I was about three years
old. My first teacher proper I identified in later years as Athena of the

Greeks, who is a very powerful tutelary deity. When you are growing up it is very difficult to cope with being different, so when I was about 14 I shut it all off. I didn't want to be involved in that other world, I wanted to be here.

The trigger for me was my eldest son, who became ill with viral encephalitis when he was three and a half months old and as a result suffered residual brain damage. He was diagnosed as being intellectually handicapped. The doctors told me that he would never be able to walk or talk and would have to spend his life in a wheelchair. I found this very difficult to accept, particularly that he was mentally handicapped, because I knew he had a remarkable sense of humour. At a very young age he understood lots of jokes, which to me indicated he had more intelligence, in terms of cognitive ability, than you would expect of an intellectually handicapped child.

That activated me to find other alternatives. I started looking at gemstones and crystals because when I was little I used to spend a lot of time on the beach looking for rocks and shells, and I had quite an impressive mineral collection. So it was natural for me to use an earth-related healing technique, such as crystals.

I experimented using different gemstones around Jim, to see if they made any difference. One I used in particular was a beautiful, deep violet stone called sugilite, which I'd read was very good for the nervous system. In New Zealand at that time it was only possible to get a couple of clear quartz crystals and amethysts; sugilite was unavailable. However, a friend of mine who went to England came back with a piece of sugilite, and I began holding this on the back of Jim's head sometimes, while I cradled him in my arms.

He began to improve. We did a lot of physiotherapy-type exercise with him as well; hitting at every level — physical, emotional and spiritual — is very much part of my philosophy, whether it be in healing or in ritual magic techniques. My son is now very much able to walk and talk and he is not retarded. He is blind and has cerebral palsy, but this is so minimal as to be no longer noticeable.

So I suppose you could say that mothering was the thing that first brought me into my own spirituality and awakened me to those things I had closed off for so many years because they frightened me. I developed my crystal healing from there and began to practise. That led me onto other fields because as I connected with the healing energies it also reopened a lot of things.

In the situation with my son what I was basically doing was using the events of my life to link in with my inner wisdom — the Gnostic wisdom, the concept of past life recall. The purpose of past life recall is to find information you have been unable to find anywhere else, to go back and have a look and remember for yourself.

So while I was working with Jim I would be remembering a lot of other things. My main access key was through my knowledge of mythology, which helped me understand the nature of archetypes and how important they were. As a child I'd had a great interest in mythologies from all over the world, and I'd spent a lot of time studying holy books from various religions — I was quite a studious little thing.

I found the most lucid description of the process by which I worked with Jim in a book by a woman called D. J. Conway. She describes it as the 'woman shaman syndrome', saying the purpose of the shaman is to travel between the worlds. I think that's true; the concept of the shaman, a unisex term and a very ancient term which transcends gender, exists in most traditions. The paths that opened to me most strongly were Greek, Egyptian and Celtic, as they were available to me through my bloodlines. I think that each time we are incarnated the DNA, which is an extraordinarily complex thing, devotes large amounts to storing records of every experience of the soul; when working in the shamanistic state one learns to dance the 'spiral dance' and move between the dimensions at will, so that past, present and future become one continuous line. So when I speak of reincarnations I mean that that is what I used in order to go back to those lifetimes where I had synthesised great amounts of information.

I had a career in television when we had only two children, though we have four now. We decided that parenting was probably more important than careers. So I left my job and came home to look after my boys, at which point I decided I would study ritual magic. I've never had a human teacher, all my teaching having been through a series of masters — masters being, of course, a unisex term.

I proceeded to study the ritual techniques of the Western Esoteric tradition and found a lot of the Christian overlay a little distasteful so I moved beyond that and connected in with my own guides and teachers and formulated my own ritual practice. This took me into Egypt and I have spent seven or eight years in communication with those deities, if you want to call them that, who teach these things.

I learned to travel through different layers of consciousness. Most of the traditions that I have looked at come back to one particular line: that of Odin of the Rune Masters, Fraya of the Vanir, back through into Greece, where the energy manifests as Hermes the son of Maia who is the eldest daughter of the seven sisters of the Pleiades, the daughters of Atlas. The third major line went back to Tahuti of Egypt, who said he in turn was the consort of the mighty Maati, who is the geneatrix of the Egyptian system.

My teachers have been the archetypes that permeate all these systems and indeed I believe the spiritual teachers of humanity are the cosmic essence of themselves. We're very diluted in this dimension in terms of light energy; they are radiant sources, so they are very pure streams of energy. No matter what system of mythology you look at, these archetypes clearly exist and they speak to us on numerous levels.

The Keeper of the Path that I have followed is a being who is known as Hermes Thrice Greatest, an androgyne energy who is defined as mind and is associated very closely with the great matriarchal mother of the system, to whom he is in service according to most of his own histories; he is usually acknowledged as her consort and he manifests as being very well balanced and is clearly able to appear as male or female.

I FOUND A LOT OF THE CHRISTIAN OVERLAY A LITTLE DISTASTEFUL SO I MOVED BEYOND THAT AND CONNECTED IN WITH MY OWN GUIDES AND TEACHERS.

My teachers have taught me how to use colour, light and sound to form cohesive images and to use these to assist others to make their own connections back into this archetypal level of consciousness. For example, I spent the last seven or eight years studying the magical traditions of ancient Egypt. It was a culture which was very clear in terms of the importance of understanding the transition into the after-life, as they called it. I studied one of the documents that came out of that time, which was a papyrus script that had been made up of a lot of different books and was basically called *The Book of Tahuti Pert em Khu*. The language is very difficult, because the translator, who was a very accurate archaeologist, acknowledges he didn't understand a lot of the spiritual keys he was translating, so this of course causes some difficulty.

I made myself very familiar, spell by spell, with the contents of the book until I got to the point where I could go through the sequences and observe what was happening. Reference points were provided, but I was able to explore on my own. From that I connected in with one of the things I am finding extremely rewarding in this incarnation – being able to work with people who are dying.

I used what I had learned in my Egyptian work to create guided meditations, shamanistic journeys, like Hermes the Psycho Pomp, who is supposed to be a leader of souls, which is the energy I work: a leader of souls walks beside people and acts as guide in the journeying between the worlds.

I use the same sort of visualisation techniques in ritual work, with various mythologies and mythological stories as guidelines and signposts to assist us along the way in this journey.

What I've also learned to do is discern within these systems which ones have essentially come down to us through patriarchal means, that is, the Christian Church and before that the Roman bureaucracy and the might of Rome that suppressed certain aspects of mythologies. If you keep your mind open to the stories you are able to understand the mother energy that has always been there, but been veiled.

I use a combination of magical, ritual and visualisation techniques to move beyond those veils and into the next level, the next dimension. You don't have to die to get there: in our own fairy stories, legends and myths we have all the keys we need, I believe, to travel back to our own forbears.

I've formulated what I call a Pathworking System, whereby I take people through the various layers of consciousness, using for each layer a tutelary deity. I perceive this as very much an empowering process for them. It's what I call the Way of the Warrior – a unisex term – and the purpose is to allow people to connect.

I work mostly with women, although about two to three percent of my students are male. I make it very clear that the systems I teach are matriarchal. The energies I have connected with are pretty much androgynous and they've told me that now is the time for the rebalancing of the masculine and the feminine. We have to work really hard to connect in with the consciousness of the mother earth, Gaia, because if we don't we will be wiped out. This is essentially the message I've been given and as I have children I have a vested interest in the future.

What spirituality means to me essentially is empowerment. I am very disturbed at how many people give away their power, especially women, and I think it is because we are programmed to do this from a really early age; we look outside ourselves. The Way of the Warrior that I teach, the Rainbow Warrior, is learning to rely upon yourself first and foremost.

Initially we have a year-long series of guided meditations, which take us through different levels. We begin on the emotional level, then move back into the subconscious level. At each of the steps, the stations along the path, we learn a different lesson. The end result of this is self-reliance, self-trust and the ability to connect and communicate with the next dimensional level.

This is basically what I've been teaching for seven or eight years and I am now moving through into the Greek system. I teach the ancient Egyptian and Greek mythologies and the ritual techniques of both of these, as well as basic ritual technique crystal healing.

Another branch of my work is helping terminally ill people. I've been very fortunate to meet up with a doctor here in Wellington who's done a lot of work with Elisabeth Kübler-Ross. We work with people who are dying, and with people who are terminally ill with cancer and Aids. This is part of my work which I find extremely joyous. It connects back into my Egyptian and Greek teachers, Anubis and Hermes. I use my crystals with this work. Essentially, I help to prepare the person for the journey they're about to undertake, which is done through a series of meetings. I usually work with the person once a week and following that I visit them.

...WORKING IN THE NFIP MOVEMENT I CAME TO UNDERSTAND FOR THE FIRST TIME HOW I WAS PART OF A PROCESS THAT COLONISED MAORI IN THIS LAND.

When a person is dying their auric field comes closer to the physical body, so it's a matter of bringing that in and opening ways for these people and making sure their transition is as easy as possible. For those who are open I do a lot of visualisation work and connecting work. I take them for example to various temples and places where they are able to connect with whatever energy they need to feel comfortable. Essentially it is a process of trying to alleviate a lot of fear.

I see it as a form of mid-wifery because I do a lot of work with babies and children and pregnant mothers as well, carrying out the traditional feminine roles. Women hold the gateways to life and death in our physical bodies, which I think is why women traditionally work in these fields.

I see it as spiritual mid-wifery, a spiritual rebirth.

I'm a Virgo: I express everything in practical terms, so spirituality for me exists in my work. I see quite a wide section of the community in what I do, whether I am teaching people how to use crystals and gemstones or how to heal themselves and others; whether I am taking them on a spiritual journey, a little trek, or working with them when they're at a time of crisis in their lives. And I think it is learning about myself through mothering my children that has been the most powerful force in my life.

I'M A VIRGO:
I EXPRESS EVERYTHING
IN PRACTICAL TERMS,
SO SPIRITUALITY
FOR ME EXISTS
IN MY WORK.

Women themselves are their own worst enemies. I know if someone says to me, 'What do you do?' and I say, 'I'm a mother,' there's a glazed look in their eyes — and it's not just men who do it. I believe this disrespect for what I consider to be my greatest vocation is a symptom of what is wrong with the human race. If people don't respect their mothers, what is there? In the same way, we don't respect the earth any more. I think there has to be a huge shift in consciousness towards the energy of the mother and the power of woman. This is what I try to bring across. I'm very clear in all my classes that this is a matriarchal system. We base everything on the lunar 13.

In terms of inspiration I've never been fortunate enough to have a human teacher and if some people find that really difficult to accept, then so be it — I've always been taught by archetypal beings. They've taught me that if you look into any system you will find the same basic energy. It's been quite interesting from that perspective. I've discovered the universality of the beings with which I work; I can go into pretty much any system now and feel comfortable because I am able to recognise them wherever they happen to be expressing themselves.

When I'm taking my classes I try not to be too sectarian; I give cross-references for people. If we are working with the energy of Artemis, we look at Baast of Egypt and at other cultures, studying the lunar aspects there.

I think the main triggers for my own spirituality have been adversity. Having had a very difficult childhood I guess that has given me inner strength. I believe that is true of most people: when you go into grief – and I've seen this a lot in my work with the dying and their relatives – it strips away all the illusions and leaves you with the bare bones. So I'd probably have to say that suffering has been my most powerful mentor.

A few years ago I was handed a piece of paper about a large gathering of people in the Yucatan in Mexico, who were being called by the Snake Lord to re-open the sacred centres there. I've always been a little dubious of foreigners coming in to 'open' this or that. But the fact that this was an indigenous shaman and it was fulfilling a prophecy made 500 years ago, made me speak to my mentors.

I've always had an affinity with the snake and the serpent, which are very powerful symbols of the feminine powers of magic in all the magical traditions. I didn't have the money or any means by which I was to go, so I threw it up to them and said, All right, if I'm meant to be there – manifest it. Within 10 days I had the money and was heading off for the Yucatan Peninsula in Mexico.

...IN TERMS OF REAL INSPIRATION I'VE FOUND AOTEAROA THE MOST POWERFUL PLACE TO BE.

I'd never had any real yearning to go anywhere else. Even though I've studied the Egyptians and the Greeks I feel those places are no longer as they were when I knew them, as I have a pretty good recall of my past re-incarnations. I feel only a great sense of sadness at the loss of those civilisations, so I'd probably weep the whole time I was over there. Anyway, I went to Mexico and had a profound awareness of what was actually happening and when I came back it opened up a whole new dimension for me; especially the teachings of a gentleman by the name of Pacau Votan who was a priest king. The Mayans had priest kings similar to the Egyptians and they built phenomenal pyramids. Just walking through miles of rainforest and seeing hills on the other side and realising they were not actually hills, but pyramids, brought me in touch with the Mayan Pleiadian energies in a way I wouldn't have believed possible.

So when I returned I was inspired to teach the Greek system, which is what I've been doing over the past few years, reformulating that and also studying the Hermetic traditions of magic.

But in terms of real inspiration I've found Aotearoa the most powerful place to be. When I started to reformulate the Egyptian system into something that most people could understand, as it's a highly technical system, I spent a lot of time at Taupo in a little settlement on the side of the lake. I was struck as I went through the Book of the Dead, where there was a map of the promised land, like the Greek Elysian Fields, to see that Taupo, when it is seen from the air, resembles this place from Egyptian mythology.

It just blew me away. I would have visions in a way that you don't normally have. A lot of people say they have visions with their third eye; well, when I'm up there I see visions with my physical eyes, things like walls of light washing down. So it really hit home to me when Tahuti, or Toff, as s/he/it is known, told me about Wellington in particular being a place that he was now, and that a lot of the civilising energies of the world were actually here in Aotearoa. In terms of the rest of the world it is a very pure place. He maintains that this country is the remains of the continent of Lemuria, a civilisation which preceded Atlantis, and all the Lemurian souls which have been instrumental in civilising and assisting humanity are here now. That is why New Zealand is such a special place.

Most of us are aware of the story of Atlantis, the remnants having come to us through Plato, through the Maya, through any of those energies that are aligned to the Pleiadian system. In Maori tradition, according to Rose Pere, who is a Maori shaman of great power whom I met once, the Pleiades played a very important part in their magical traditions. The Mayans and the Greeks also placed a great deal of importance on the Pleiades as well.

So we know about Atlantis, aside from all the flood mythologies permeating the whole of the collective unconsciousness which come out in so many different cultures and stories. Atlantis was preceded by another vast civilisation known as Lemuria. The Druids remember Lemuria as 'Mu', and Atlantis as 'Is'. They speak of the lands of the east and the west.

The Lemurians were I suppose the forerunners of Homo sapiens. They appear to have been semi-divine; they were the Titans, the fabulous magicians and heroes of old that different cultures seem generally to agree once existed. They were still very conscious of the elements at that time and of fairies, sylphs, dryads, elves and all those sorts of beings that were still around. This was called the golden race or the golden times. Most cultures attribute the end of this race to the wrath of God, but I think the Goddess became fed up with them, shrugged her shoulders, rearranged the mantle of the ocean which covers her, and simply swamped them – flushed them away. That was the mighty flood. Lemuria disappeared completely and all that remains of it are this country, Australia and the islands of the Pacific and there's a very special energy here because the diva spirits are strong.

Very few of the Atlantean civilisations survived. They set up outposts in various places in the world – in South America, Egypt, Britain and on Easter Island. They taught us the basics of magic ritual and they understood the real power of the mind; but because we have been taught by Atlantans we 'Westerners' tend to think of things in terms of technology.

After these civilisations, humanity was then perfected and given a vast technology and the training to use it, adapted from the more organic Lemurian into a highly sophisticated, crystal-based technology – a silicon-based technology.

It's interesting how people of the white race are generally referred to as 'Westerners'. Is this a backlash from American imperialism or it true as it was prophesied? In *The Egyptian Book of the Dead* there are a lot of references to the Westerners, not all of them very nice as the Westerners tended to be feared.

New Zealand has been inhabited for a very short space of time; I don't wish to enter into any controversies, but in terms of land being inhabited a couple of thousand years is but the blink of an eye. So the land still has a pristine purity about it. I believe we are very fortunate to be living here, because we are the first people in the world to see the sun. For most of the major religions, in terms of ritual that is an extraordinary place to be. In Mexico this was one of the things I was able to share with them. We are the first place to greet Hun'ab Ku, as they call the central intelligence of the universe, which is represented to them by the sun. As we are the first people in the world to greet the sun it is almost as if we are the keepers of the gateways. There are so many places in this country which are remarkably potent I have no need or desire to travel anywhere else, because I know it is all here.

It seems to be typical of New Zealanders to think that everybody overseas knows everything and we don't, but what struck me when I was overseas was that although they had conferences with really well-known authors speaking, these people weren't making any huge revelations that I wasn't already aware of. It empowered me tremendously. I believe we have everything we need here – all the teachers, the healers, the magicians; all we need do is ask.

It's been my mission in life to empower people to understand that point; to see that they don't really have to come and see me because they have everything they need within themselves. Like a good mother, I try to teach people as I teach my own children: to be independent, to give them the tools they need to live their lives and to instil in them some understanding of nurture.

I see myself constantly evolving. When I look back at notes I've made at classes from 10 years back I find I've evolved tremendously. I think I've become more simple in how I try to transmit my information to others. I try to give people the very basic guidelines, such as who is at east, west, south, north and what elements represent these areas. I say to them, 'The whole point of this process is to empower you, so you can create your own rituals.'

THEY MUST MAKE THEIR OWN RITUALS BECAUSE I THINK THE WORST THING ORGANISED RELIGION HAS DONE IS MAKE US RELY ON PRIESTS.

They must make their own rituals because I think the worst thing organised religion has done is make us rely on priests. So I'm very careful to ensure that people who come to my classes are aware that I am basically a scholar who likes to talk — I am not a guru. To me these are very male concepts and very disempowering.

My aim for the future is to continue to raise people's consciousness of the mother energy. I shall continue to learn and grow and I hope hold up the light for other people to see where they can head for.

Our cultures are so rich and diverse in spirituality. I have a background in Celtic, Slavic, Germanic and English druidic traditions. When we think in terms of Western spirituality we think of Christianity, but we have hugely rich traditions. We have the Western esoteric tradition which has been going on since time immemorial.

There was one thing that happened to me in Mexico which I found quite distasteful. At the end of a talk they did a kind of a play that represented the tribes of humanity. The black was earth, the brown was the emotions, the red were spirituality, the yellow was the mind. Then came whitey, this horrible grasping, sterile thing that couldn't exist without the others; that was true, but I didn't like the way it was portrayed. I found it so distasteful I left, because I believe it's a stereotype; it's totally untrue and it denies the underlying force of our traditions.

I've spoken to various energies about the 'white tribe', and they said our function is transformation. We are the sub-sect of humanity that creates change. No one likes change and we are afraid of it, but one of my favourite phrases in class is, 'The only constant is change.'

Of course, in that respect we are to be feared; but to state that we have no spirituality of our own is to deny thousands and thousands of years of magical tradition. I think we are more into the mind than we are into the heart. In fact, the Hermetic tradition is based on the mind. We have no idea of the power of the mind; just look at what people achieve through visualisation techniques in their own self-transformation.

I think we need to come together to share more. Tahuti has stated everybody must now come forward; there is no more time for secret societies and secret traditions. The time is now for the whole of the race to come together, to weave in harmony and sing in harmony to the creative energies. Another reason I feel so moved to teach it is that the more people who are open to it and aware, the better.

I use a lot of sonics in my work. There's a real reason for this. For a start the Hermetic tradition is based largely on sonics, particularly on chanting. The priesthood in the Christian churches only allowed people to chant in church because they understood the power of the word, the power of chanting. They told this to generation upon generation, but they weren't interested in empowering, only in disempowerment.

So maybe this is where the idea that Westerners have no souls has come from, because you find in most other traditions there is a lot of chanting and a lot of sound. If we go along with the idea that the Hermetics and the Egyptians teach, and that the Christians themselves borrowed from *The Egyptian Book of the Dead*, 'In the beginning was the word,' we accept the universe was created with a word. It shows us how vitally important sound is.

I think we Westerners have to learn again. I think the sooner people realise how simple it is to reconnect with superconscious levels, the better for everyone. The challenge I think for women, in the field of shamanistic practice, is to re-establish contact with the universal mother consciousness in all her aspects: Maiden, Mother and Crone. Women are able to realign themselves in this manner because we hold the gateways to life and death within ourselves, within our physical bodies. I think we accelerate the shifts in consciousness for others because we are the creator force of humanity. We have forgotten that fact and been brainwashed into not acknowledging it; we sustain and nurture life, we give birth and we die. This makes us, women, the natural shamans.

Because women are the mothers, the teachers and the nurturers, we are the ones who shape our society, and we need to teach our children again how to find their voices and how to sing and to sing to the universe in joy. There's nothing quite like it.

Comparatively speaking, Western women have a lot more choices than many other cultures. We have a lot of religious freedom and I believe we have through our mythologies the keys to our own spiritual paths if we have chosen not to accept the patriarchal teachings of the church. (I do know though of Christian women who explore with complete freedom other aspects of their cultural heritage, so this is not just restricted to the Pagan – for want of a better word – system.)

The fact that we have won for ourselves so many freedoms and set an example culturally in terms of our social freedom and our democratic rights means we are acknowledging the place of mother and women in society. The Mother Goddess is arising and it is an awesome sight.

HELEN POLLOCK

THREE IMPOSING FACES LOOK DOWN FROM THE SIDEBOARD: THE GUARDIANS,
LARGE, PIT-FIRED CLAY PIECES, ARE REMINDERS TO US TO CONSIDER
THE DIRECTION THAT LIFE IS TAKING.
THESE FACES HAVE THE CHARACTERISTIC STRENGTH OF POTTER
AND SCULPTOR HELEN POLLOCK'S WORK. SHE LIVES ON
AUCKLAND'S NORTH SHORE AND HAS SPENT SEVERAL YEARS
WORKING — FULL TIME SINCE 1985 — IN A STUDIO SET UP IN A
CONVERTED GARAGE IN HER BACK GARDEN, USING LOW-TECH
FIRING METHODS.
HER WORK IS VERY MUCH AN EXPRESSION OF HER SPIRITUALITY
AND HAS GROWN OUT OF HER INTENSE AND MAJOR LIFE EXPERIENCES.

She studied design and attended painting and pottery classes at Otago Polytechnic while at school in Dunedin and extended this through an applied design and art history course, which included ceramic and fibre art, while studying for a home science degree at Otago University.

Her work has been exhibited in New Zealand in group and solo exhibitions and has won national recognition. It has also been exhibited in Canada and California. Television New Zealand's Kaleidoscope programme on New Zealand art featured her work several times and she was interviewed as one of five artists in a National Radio series of programmes about New Zealand artists entitled 'The Spirit in Their Art'.

Brought up in Dunedin and influenced by a strongly Presbyterian family, Helen went to Sunday School and Bible Class until she was about 18 years old. She left Dunedin when she was 20, to go to teachers' college in Auckland, where she later taught at a secondary school.

I became aware of the hypocrisy that can be present in a church and became pretty angry with the whole church. However, I still went every now and then.

I was married in a church and had my children christened but I found it inadequate for dealing with some of the things I was trying to cope with at the time. I had expected to be able to go there in times of need and when it didn't deliver I became cynical about spirituality in general and cut off from it.

My father died when I was nine. It took me two years to believe he had definitely died and was not coming back. I decided then that I was basically on my own. My mother did not communicate with me emotionally the way I needed to be communicated with and at that point the real me went inside and became secret because it seemed I had nobody to communicate with.

I felt if anybody knew what I was thinking I would be isolated so I acted on the outside as everybody expected me to be – pleasant but superficial.

I remember having a conversation with my brother when I was 11, when I decided that what I wanted from life was to have lots of ups and downs and have people close to me die or relationships to change and break up – a dramatic kind of life, so that when I was old I'd be able to look back and think I had really lived life to the hilt. Also, at that age I decided I wanted to be a potter and a sculptor. It's as if I was really clear then, but lost myself as I became older and when I got married.

There were five years of trauma. I married, my mother died and my second baby died. I coped by battening down the hatches and functioning like a robot through those years, mainly because I thought nobody would understand. When I got to the age of 35 my marriage broke up and I thought I was going to die if I didn't break out of where I was, which was a really closed-in box.

All those years I kept thinking back to the conversation I had had when I was 11: that this was what I wanted and what I had got. Trying to make sense of all the grief over my father, my mother, my child, and my marriage as well, pushed me into being an artist and into the realisation of my spirituality.

I was catapulted into a period of intense introspection resulting in some insights. I saw I was seeking experience, but indiscriminately, and then passively using pain as an escape for not living fully. I think of it now as avoiding joy. I used to think life was hard and suffering would make me a better person — which it can do.

Later I could see I was choosing to make everything difficult for myself — becoming, as Van Morrison put it, 'high on the art of suffering'. And of course with all that suffering I couldn't begin to express who I truly was.

Then I went through a phase of thinking, We create our own reality and 'choose' to be happy. What I think now is that the issue is to be open to what has meaning, to answer the 'gentle knock at the door', to risk being fully with my life however it unfolds — the pain and the pleasure. That's joy: to listen to the small, still voice that says, 'Do it!' It's about allowing time to be with that voice 'which speaks most loudly in the stillness and the silence broken only by birdsong'.

I find the slow, repetitive building with clay, as people have for centuries, is like a meditation — the clay and my hands 'do it' while I watch.

Having been pushed back to virtual psychic death, now life feels like one long, awesome, amazing thing.

Around the time my marriage broke up I used to sit and look at myself in the mirror. It was like getting used to who I was — coming back into myself. When I split up I had no idea what I looked like or what I wanted and for about two years I sat in front of a mirror several times a day.

I think that's what a lot of my faces are about — that straight look, very focused and still, coming

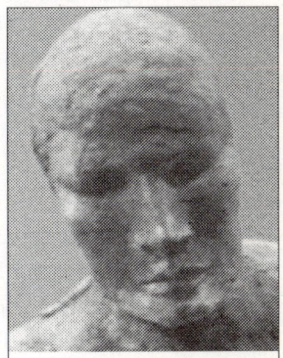

TRYING TO MAKE SENSE OF ALL THE GRIEF OVER MY FATHER, MY MOTHER, MY CHILD, AND MY MARRIAGE AS WELL, PUSHED ME INTO BEING AN ARTIST AND INTO THE REALISATION OF MY SPIRITUALITY.

from within. Each one is integrating some aspect of myself. All the work that I do is me and the fact that other people respond to it is wonderful. That's great, but basically it is for me. It's my way of making sense of my reality.

I was using pain in my life to avoid taking responsibility to truly live and experience all of my life — passion and joy. Then the realisation took place over several years where I started to see my life as a journey to my divine self. That's when I began to move into a more formal kind of spirituality.

In the early eighties I became involved with collaborative installation work with other women, working with fibre and other materials. The three installations were facilitated by Juliet Batten. Gradually I became more absorbed in my own work, choosing clay as a medium. I've always enjoyed working with clay: it is sensual, responsive and seems to contain infinite possibilities. I enjoy the fact that it is such an ancient material and that people have been making clay objects since pre-history.

To fire the way I do – placing the work back in its origin, the earth, lighting a huge fire over it, controlling the amount of wind and watching for the rain – seems a totally appropriate way to complete my work. The marks of the fire are clearly visible and are an integral part of the completed work.

Juliet Batten inspired me to move from doing my art as a hobby to taking it up full time. But in any case for me it was like a compulsion because of how my life had evolved: I wanted to express my life. It's been a cathartic thing, like a volcano.

I used to go to Te Henga a lot to stay at Juliet's bach, just to stare at the sky and be alone. I think I could have sped the whole process up if I had been on my own, but I had three children to look after, which was good for me, really – practical and grounding, giving me a lot of work to do every day, a lot to think about. Also at the time I was developing myself as an artist.

For nine years I was too busy coping with everyday life to bother about spirituality. I didn't even consider it was an issue, so it's interesting the way it came flooding in again and it's so important to me now. It was through the collaborative art work that I began the connection with my spirituality and started creating rituals. Eventually I became a part of a group called Cone. For me art and ritual overlap; they both bring into consciousness the intangible.

I find conventional spirituality is so male dominated I cannot relate to it. That's why I have taken up women's spirituality and why I do visual art that contains images of women. It feels like the ultimate intrusion to make an image of one's spirituality and for it always to be masculine. It's very denigrating to women – as if we can't be divine.

My art is political in that sense. It's empowering for women to have images of women as strong, divine beings, and generating change in the viewer is also very empowering.

My first solo exhibition 'Ritual' in 1986 explored the feminine through making clay masks of various aspects of Mother Goddess archetypes: Kali, Athene and Selene, decorating them with shells, seagrass and horsehair.

'Reconstructing' in 1988 was again an exploration of the feminine – Jung's 'anima' aspect of the self – visiting the woundedness and neglectedness to reconstruct and heal, remembering and reclaiming feminine archetypes: the Daughter Persephone, the Mother Demeter and the Crone, the Wise Old Woman of matriarchal mythology.

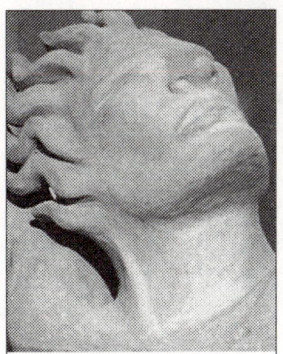

THEMES OF BIRTH
AND FULFILMENT,
DEATH AND REBIRTH
AS EXPRESSED
IN MYTH AND
SYMBOLS REALLY
INTEREST ME.

This second solo exhibition evolved from a dream I had in which I was carrying a gift from myself to two friends and I accidentally dropped it into an overflowing sewer, guarded by a horrible rat. I decided I could not retrieve the gift and went on to see the couple with a profound sense of disappointment that I would not have all of myself for them and would only be able to describe what I had left behind in the sewer.

My work has been to enter the sewer, the underworld – the unconscious – to retrieve my gift, a lost part of myself, and to reconstruct it. The masks are a point between the inner and outer worlds. They are sometimes whole, sometimes fragments of archetypal beings, sometimes female; others are androgynous. In this exhibition I was working on understanding and integrating the feminine archetypes of the Daughter Persephone, the Mother Demeter, Artemis the independent woman and Kali the Destroyer.

The exhibition included works entitled 'Wounded Vessels' and 'Abandoned Vessels' – pit-fired figures that are vessels for arriving and departing, the vessel being the container of the soul. The bodies are torn and wounded, but in essence they are indestructible and seeking wholeness. In these pieces I was seeking a balance between masculine Logos – technology and materialism – and the feminine Eros and appreciation of the wisdom of the natural law.

Themes of birth and fulfilment, death and rebirth as expressed in myth and symbols really interest me.

In 1990 a QEII Arts Council grant enabled me to install 'Storehouse' in the ASA Gallery and again in the Fisher Gallery sculpture court in

1991. To enter the storehouse is to enter your body, your temple.
Everything comes here to be gathered together, sorted and sifted, and the
finest is offered up in gratitude and to ensure continuity.

The exhibit included the 'Vessel for Entering' (now in St George's
Presbyterian Church, Takapuna) and seven grinding stones, symbols for
transformation and also representing seven energy centres for the body.

These lay on the floor before a large 'Altar' with an
earthy-looking Goddess reaching upwards to a cres-
cent moon. On the side were 'Seven Receptacles':
vessels which bring their contents to the 'Storehouse'
and are taken away, to begin again.

In 1994 and 1995 I curated two exhibitions entitled 'Spiritual Themes in Art' at St George's in which
I invited artists to show works exploring a wide range
of spiritual perspectives and expressions.

And in 1994 I exhibited at Chiaroscuro Gallery,
Auckland. The exhibit was called 'Craving Images', in
which I explored my own need, and what seems a
universal and ancient desire, to make contact with
beyond and in some way to 'hold' the insight.

...TO MOVE MORE
DEEPLY INTO
OURSELVES, EXPRESS
OURSELVES MORE
FULLY AND SEE IT
AS A CHALLENGE
TO LIVE MORE
DEEPLY.

I think ancient hand-held clay figurines, the magnificence of a cathedral or a temple, or a simple way-
side shrine are examples of this craving.

My recent work is called 'Observance', as in observance of the soul. They are life-sized figures 'caught
in the moment' or maybe glimpsing the transcendent.
I think it is important to allow space in our lives to
tend our souls and allow time to notice 'the still point
between' to validate our soul life and to spend time
nurturing that connection.

My children, two sons and a daughter, are resistant to any overt ritual-
making, but they are taking it in through my art. When my oldest son
was 13 he got quite angry about all my art being about women. He could
sense it was quite political, but he's starting to accept it now.

Rituals have been a powerful part of my life. A ritual I did for my son
David, who died, was incredibly healing. It took me about 11 years to
carry out the ritual, because before that I didn't feel able. Until I did it
I couldn't talk about him. The ritual made a celebration of his life.

The real beauty of it was planning it and thinking out what it meant to me. Once I had planned the ritual, doing it was almost secondary as I had got to the space I needed. Basically it was about letting him go, which I hadn't done, and actually celebrating the learning around his whole life and death.

There had been things, like, I felt sorry for myself; why had this terrible thing happened to me? By that time I was able to see his life and death as a privilege.

More recently I did a death ritual that I wanted to repeat again and again. Stones and little white shells that looked like tiny bones were laid in a circle on a black cloth on the floor and within it a ring of candles. We moved the stones and shells across the candles into the centre, describing each with a word of what death was: 'ugly', 'final', 'peaceful'; doing it over and over again until we put them all in the centre. Here they were contained both physically, in terms of the ritual space, and psychologically, in the context of the process of the ritual.

Then we put into this container our stories of death, individual stories of death, physical or otherwise. We put a symbol of death into the container and did a meditation on death – the death of a relationship, an idea – and we were all invited to see it as a call from the Goddess to move more deeply into ourselves, express ourselves more fully and see it as a challenge to live more deeply.

Just preparing the ritual made me feel fantastic – everything glistened with life. It's so life-enhancing to face up to something difficult. Before, I was too terrified to face things; I was afraid that if I lifted the lid I would be annihilated.

ACKNOWLEDGEMENTS

I'd like to thank

✧   each of the women interviewed in this book: firstly for sharing their experiences with me, then for the time they gave me to be interviewed, and finally for the time they took to read the text of their interviews — for some this process happened over several years

✧   Joan Jones and Diana Hibberd who, at different stages, contributed to reading the text and making suggestions for its development

✧   Cathie Dunsford, who supported the idea, made suggestions and worked on the interviews with such energy and enthusiasm

✧   Linda Hill for the use of her computer in the early stages

✧   Nicholas Morton for help with my own computer — and for his telephone explanations answering my questions at any time of the night or day

✧   all of my friends and family who patiently listened and then supported me through the ideas and processes of these interviews

✧   Diana Harris for her editorial work on the manuscript, Sally Hollis-McLeod for the design of the book, and Helen Pollock for allowing us to reproduce her work on the front and back cover

✧   Bob Ross, Helen Benton and Renée Lang at Tandem for publishing the book.

BIBLIOGRAPHY

BANCROFT, ANNE *Weavers of Wisdom: Women Mystics of the Twentieth Century*. Arkana, 1989.

BATTEN, JULIET *Celebrating the Southern Seasons: Rituals for Aotearoa*. Tandem Press, 1995.

BATTEN, JULIET *Power from Within: A Feminist Guide to Ritual Making*. Ishtar Books, 1988.

BOND, WILLIAM AND SHEFFIELD, PAMELA *The Gospel of the Goddess*. Artemis Creations Publishing, 1984.

CAMERON, ANNE *Daughters of Copperwoman*. Women's Press, 1984.

CAUFIELD OCSM, SEAN *The Experience of Praying*. Paulist Press, USA 1980.

COOK, CATHERINE AND VON SAMMARUGA, DWARIKO *Songs for the Journey Home – A Pacific Tarot Deck and Book*. Artists and Alchemists Press, 1994.

DALY, MARY *The Church and the Second Sex*. Beacon Press (re-issued), 1985.

DOHERTY, CATHERINE DE HUEK *Poustinia*. Ave Maria Press, 1975.

DUNSFORD, CATHIE *Cowrie*. Tandem Press, 1994.

DUNSFORD, CATHIE *The Journey Home: Te Haerenga Kainga*. Spinifex Press, 1997.

DUNSFORD, CATHIE *Survivors: Uberlebende*. University of Osnabruck Press, 1990.

FERGUSON, M. *The Aquarian Conspiracy*. Tarcher, 1987.

GREER, GERMAINE *The Female Eunuch*. Grafton,1971.

MARIECHILDS, DIANE *Motherwit*. Crossing Press, 1981.

PENNY, NOREEN *Women's Rites: An Alternative to Patriarchal Religion*. 1994.

REDFORD, JAMES *The Celestine Prophecy*. Satori Publishing, 1993.

STARHAWK *The Spiral Dance*. Harper and Row, 1979.

SPRETNAK, SHARLENE *The Politics of Women's Spirituality*. Anchor Press Doubleday, 1982.

STEIN, DIANE *The Kwan Yin Book of Changes*. Llewellyn Publications, 1985.

STONE, MERLIN *The Paradise Papers*. Virago in association with Quartet Books, 1976.

WOODRUFF, SUE *Meditations with Mechtild of Magdeburg*. Bear and Company Inc, 1982.

ZOHAR, DANAH *The Quantum Self*. Flamingo, 1991.